JOSEPH G. BERTI

THE
BOOK
ON
SOFTWARE

THE PROVEN PATH TO SUCCESS
IN THE SOFTWARE INDUSTRY

Copyright © 2025 by Berti Ventures, LLC

The Book On Software

The Proven Path to Success in the Software Industry

All rights reserved. No part of this publication may be reproduced, distributed or transmitted in any form or by any means, including photocopying, recording, or other electronic or mechanical methods, without the prior written permission of the publisher, except in the case of brief quotations embodied in critical reviews and certain other noncommercial uses permitted by copyright law.

Although the author and publisher have made every effort to ensure that the information in this book was correct at press time, the author and publisher do not assume and hereby disclaim any liability to any party for any loss, damage, or disruption caused by errors or omissions, whether such errors or omissions result from negligence, accident, or any other cause.

Adherence to all applicable laws and regulations, including international, federal, state and local governing professional licensing, business practices, advertising, and all other aspects of doing business in the US, Canada or any other jurisdiction is the sole responsibility of the reader and consumer.

Neither the author nor the publisher assumes any responsibility or liability whatsoever on behalf of the consumer or reader of this material. Any perceived slight of any individual or organization is purely unintentional.

The resources in this book are provided for informational purposes only and should not be used to replace the specialized training and professional judgment of a lawyer or legal professional.

Neither the author nor the publisher can be held responsible for the use of the information provided within this book. Please always consult a trained professional before making any decision regarding treatment of yourself or others.

ISBN: 979-8-89109-729-2 - paperback
ISBN: 979-8-89109-730-8 - ebook
ISBN: 979-8-89109-731-5 - hardcover

DEDICATION

To all of the people who have been in the trenches launching software solutions with me. My journey in the software industry would not be the same if I only considered the software we created together. Software becomes outdated, the journey and memories are timeless.

And to you, the reader, for making the journey of writing The Book On Software worthwhile. You breathe life into these pages and are living the life of a person who ships software, seemingly making the impossible possible.

TABLE OF CONTENTS

Dedication	iii
Introduction	1
Getting Started	7
The Top 5	12
Why Does Your Company Exist?	14
Misguided Why Case Study	18
The Software Life Cycle	24
Ideation	28
Launch	29
Growth	29
Cash Cow	30
Decline	32
Re-Invest	33
Messaging	37
Messaging In Practice	41
Employment Agreements	52
Culture	55
Design, Development and Product	63
Building the Machine	64
"All In" Agile	66
Discipline for Requirements and Design	75
Product	77
Trusted Advisor	80
Established Expertise	81
Output Quality	81
Well-Baked Requirements	82

Stakeholder Communication	88
Roadmaps	88
Enhancement Requests	89
Value Maximization	89
Release Notes	89
Use Clear and Precise Language	94
Organize Requirements:	96
Be Specific	97
Use a Consistent Format	98
Use Case Map Example	99
Include Functional Requirements	101
Address Non-Functional Requirements	101
Consider Compliance and Regulatory Requirement	102
Include Interface and Integration Requirements	102
Define Clear Acceptance Criteria	103
Traceability	103
Review and Revise	103
Document Change Control	104
User story mapping	104
Product Roadmaps	105
Competitors	119
The Go-to-Market Team	**124**
Category 1	127
Category 2	129
Category 3	132
Market Sizing	135
Operating Models	138
Go-to-Market Model (GTM)	140
Usage Metering Model	142
Digital Metering Model	144
In arrears	147
Pre-billed	148
Overage billing	148
In application purchases	148
OEM billing	149

Licensing Models	149
Perpetual	149
SAAS	150
Term	151
Provisioning Model	151
Self Provisioning	152
SaaS Provisioned	152
On Premise	152
Embedded	152
Pricing Models	153
Processor	153
User	153
Install	154
Disk space	154
Consumption based	154
Design	**156**
Preparation	161
Testing	161
Observation and Feedback	162
Debriefing	162
The Design "Team"	164
Interaction Designer	164
Graphic Designer	165
Visual Designer	165
Researcher	165
Who not to hire!	166
Wireframes vs High Fidelity	167
Tiger teams	171
Sustainable design	172
Software Development	**174**
Sales	**186**
The Demo	187
The Value Process	189
Sales Talent	190
Install Base Sales	194
Sales Operations	196

Marketing	**202**
Product Pages	207
Marketing Coordination	208
Influencer marketing	213
Operations and Finance	**218**
Financial Modeling	219
Revenue recognition	221
SaaS Modelling	221
Cost and Cash Flow Modelling	222
Profitability and Product Pricing	222
Scaling	223
Metrics	225
Growth Metrics	229
Financial Metrics	230
Product Metrics	233
Legal	235
Agreement Types	236
Intellectual Property Rights	236
Assignment Rights	237
Termination Rights	238
Antitrust	238
Patents	239
Conclusion	**241**
References	**245**
Acknowledgements	**248**
About the Author	**250**

INTRODUCTION

I'm often asked about my secret sauce. Typically, the individual asking receives a smile from me, followed by a deep breath, and then the question: "Well, how much time do you have?" You see, the secret sauce they are referring to is how my software teams have produced and delivered more products to market, often in about half to one-third the time of our competitors, and with fewer people than most.

I'm not being modest, but initially, I did not realize the uniqueness of how I managed products and took them to market until I came up for a breath of air and looked at other software companies. Bogged down in more work than I could fathom, a private equity (PE) firm that had just invested in the next round of funding asked me for a list of companies in our domain that were competitors or complimentary to our software products. Eager to fulfill their request, I gave them a list of 30-plus companies without thinking much about it. Honestly, I was busy and just trying to make them go away. To my surprise, the PE firm called each company and met with their executive teams. They were priming themselves to acquire the firms on my list. I now know this process is called a roll-up and is a common growth strategy for investment firms.

Yet, much to my dismay, not only did the investors not stay out of my hair, but I was asked to attend diligence calls and other meetings as the PE firm evaluated if these companies were a fit for us. At the time, my small team and I were trying to launch a new module every 12 months. My schedule was ridiculous, to say the least. But I'm glad I went through it because what I discovered was eye-opening.

My team had less than 10 people who, within one year alone, doubled the company's total lines of code and built seven modules in eight years. So, as we reviewed our competitors and complementary businesses, it was shocking how much time these other teams—many far larger than mine—were taking to build their products. I repeatedly asked myself, "Did these companies really spend the last ten years working on *only* that?" Essentially, this experience marked my recognition of my "secret sauce." Not to mention, I also learned to ask analysts at private equity firms why they are asking for something!

As a software entrepreneur, I have worked on launching (or re-launching) over 25-plus software products. For many of these, I have directly led or was heavily involved in getting a product to market. More than half of those product launches were designed and built from the ground up—starting with a blank sheet of paper. I have also been CEO of three different software companies and was Head of Product for a

1.5 billion dollar plus software unit at IBM. There, I was directly responsible for the product team and the direction of over 20-plus products. I was so involved with these product launches that I started signing my requirements documents as "a little birdie." At a company like IBM, they were not used to a VP writing detailed software requirements so I obscured the name on the requirements document I wrote to stay under the radar of the obscure hierarchy of such a large company. I also wanted my team to challenge the requirements. These product specs wound up going sometimes to hundreds of people. I later had teams demoing products to me to give me an update where most of the people on the call did not know I wrote the original use cases and was on weekly design playbacks helping to design the software. They had no idea why I had such a big smile on my face.

Why so many software products? Well, I believe it is just how I am wired. I enjoy creating things. When I'm not launching new software products, I'm sketching designs in notebooks for things like chicken coops, a tiny house (that is now my office), a drip watering system for my orchard, or whatever else has caught my interest.

I am an entrepreneur (and as I jokingly say, otherwise unemployable!).

Now, it took me time to realize that title. Early in my career, I struggled to determine where I fit in and what

I was supposed to do with my skills because I had a unique way of working. So, during lunch with someone I respected, Jamie O'Neil, he stated, "You are an entrepreneur." I had never considered it and wasn't sure what to think. I was taken aback. He had just crashed the company he co-founded, and everyone lost their job (including me), so I did not want to be in his situation (at the time).

Admittedly, I first translated his comments as: "Joe, you are otherwise unemployable and need to figure out a creative way to employ yourself." Later, I realized Jamie had a point. I excelled in working with others who desired to work smart and produce better results than the average team. I loved the high-intensity environments with a common goal—it fit me and my skills. I took that insight and ran with it to great success.

So, when more and more people told me I should write a book, I listened, with some initial skepticism, but again, I came around to see their perspectives had merit. That is not to say I take everyone's suggestions. So please, do not get any ideas to team up on me to say I should be a circus clown. Nothing against clowns, but I know my limitations!

Additionally, I realized there were very few good books on operating a software company. As someone who devours information, I have continuously searched for something to help me develop and market my products without learning by trial and error, better known as "the hard way."

Of course, many will still use the figure-things-out-as-they-go-method, but why? If you have a resource to help you achieve success faster and with fewer downfalls, why not use it? So, as you continue, you will see this book is designed to take you through all the aspects of software development, giving you specific advice on how to design, develop, market, and ultimately gauge and maintain its success. This book is not just for the newbie; it can be for anyone at any stage of their product life cycle who is open to rethinking their approach. It's truly a tool I wish I had years ago!

Therefore, I hope this book becomes a well-worn reference for you and that it propels your software business to new heights in less time and with few, if any, pitfalls!

GETTING STARTED

My thirst for creativity has been the impetus to launching or re-launching a new product every 12 months over the past 23 years. For some of those years, I worked on multiple product launches simultaneously. Designing, developing, and delivering a new product is like running a marathon; sometimes I question how long I can continue at this pace. But then again, if you enjoy what you are doing, why stop? And just like a marathon, once you have trained, the process gets easier each time. Eventually, you reach that point where everything around you appears to be happening at a snail's pace.

This became my reality during my four years at IBM. After selling a company to them, I joined with over one billion dollars worth of software under my purview. I was Head of Product for a software unit that spanned many different teams, offerings, and industries. My position included software for everything from the supply chain, asset maintenance, building management, IoT, blockchain, the business application portion of the weather business, Watson Media, engineering software (originally Tivoli/Rational), and sustainability. My thirst for launching software applications did not get slowed down by a big company. I had more resources to launch more products than ever before. New products included Maximo Monitor, Health, Predict, and Mobile which then was delivered as the Maximo Application Suite, the Environmental Intelligence Suite, the Supply Chain Intelligence Suite, and the Digital Twin Exchange (which later became Maximo Marketplace).

As time passed, I began to see similarities in the mistakes being made by software teams. When you look under the hood of enough software offerings, the patterns reveal themselves. For starters, there were incorrectly priced products, broken messaging, and strategies misaligned with the life cycle stage of the software, and inefficient processes in the product, design, and development teams.

Understand that the software business is not for the faint of heart. You need perseverance and grit if you want to reach your goals. Therefore, I hunkered down and employed what I now call "my secret sauce" and made the necessary changes for success. That information and experience I employed at IBM and many other companies will be shared in the coming pages.

However, before we get started, please note: Within this book, you can access specific tools to help you. These tools were created over 20-plus years out of necessity. The teams I have worked with consist of intelligent people, and when I provided them with an example of what I was talking about, they learned quickly and delivered results faster. I will refer to the templates as "artifacts" throughout this content. These artifacts have aided my teams' output with a wide range of companies and products; each time they consistently produced positive outcomes.

These artifacts can be sampled for free on my website https://thebookonsoftware.com/downloads and I provide QR codes you can scan with your phone along the way. Others require a fee to download. They are also sold as a bundle if you want access to all of them. Using these templates will produce at least 25 times the return on time and monetary investment. I know this because I spent many late nights producing them for my companies, and they have paid off time and time again!

Also, at the end of each section, you will note that I have provided a series of takeaways to summarize key points. Use these sections as a checklist to ensure you are on target for whatever stage your product is in.

Let's get started!

THE TOP 5

There are five foundational areas essential to your product, sales, and operation, including finance, of any company. Becoming "world-class," requires a complete understanding of the following:

- Knowing the "why" for your product
- The software life cycle
- Winning the messaging game
- Finding and attracting the right talent
- Company culture

A misguided understanding of why your product exists will lead to both poor product-market fit and wasted time and money. Not realizing that software has a life cycle, a beginning and end, or what you do during each phase of a software's life cycle can vary immensely. We will cover the life cycle stages of a software product in the "Top 5" section of this book as it is fundamental to understanding the software business. Producing the best software but not realizing that the best messaging wins, not necessarily the best software, can lead to disappointment. A company is powered by its in-house talent, which makes hiring the right people fundamental to everything a company does.

Have the wrong people on your team? If so, you are likely on the path to failure.

Essentially, if an organization does not address these five foundational elements, nothing they do will lead to success, which is the ultimate goal, right? So let's do a deeper dive into these five areas.

Why Does Your Company Exist?

Your company and product should have a clear reason for existing. A single product can rarely be a fit for all markets – being all things to all people is unattainable. Attempting to be the end-all and be-all for your potential users will incite a lack of clarity, therefore, producing products and results that are undesirable —no one will want to use your product, and your financials will reflect that. A now famous cartoon from *The Joy of Tech* (Schmalcel & Evans, 2016) describes what would happen to a product that is trying to please everyone and has no direct reason for existing.

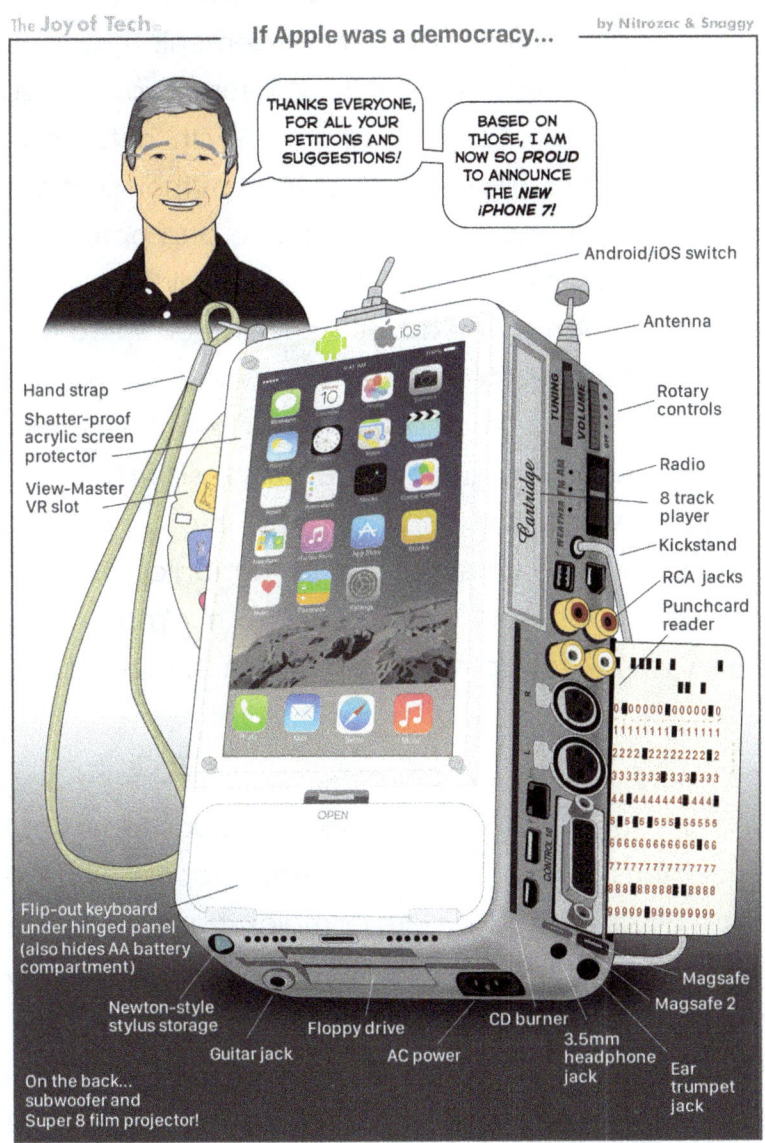

I was being pursued for a role at a private equity firm with billions of dollars under management. They were looking for in-residence entrepreneurs and noticed my product background, so I met with a team of Chief Product Officers across several of their portfolio companies. It was an interesting role and potentially lucrative. You become a member of their team, and as the companies you advise perform well, so do you. As the interview progressed, everyone seemed to be looking for a "methodology" for prioritizing what features to put into the software. Was their entire focus *really* on what features to put next into a product? They seemed to be searching for a magical formula to manage product features. Yet, to my knowledge, there is no cookie-cutter approach for prioritizing features.

It would be nice to have an out-of-the-box, sure-fire method to give to your product team that encompassed the decision-making process of Steve Jobs. However, it is far more complex than that. I have certainly leveraged feature scoring models where you weigh features based on things like revenue potential, customer value, customer pain, support savings, performance, and usability. Certainly, these weighting systems are useful tools when you deal with many products with thousands of feature requests in their backlog. However, these models do not get to the root of what the product team needs to think through.

So during the interview I answered their question on how I would prioritize what the product team worked on and my answer seemed to confuse them even more. I answered by saying that I would not only look at the features of the product but the entire GTM strategy, starting with the messaging. I would start with "why" the product exists in the first place and that it depended upon the life-cycle stage of the product (more on this later). A product that is new to the market will have a very different approach than a mature product that is 7-10 years into its life cycle. Starting with the "why" is not a new concept.

Simon Sinkek, author of the book *Start with Why* (Sinek, 2009), dives deeper into this subject. If you have not yet mastered the "Why" for your software solution, you must. For example, if the product team is out of touch with why customers are buying and using the software, they will make bad decisions and nothing else will matter—garbage in, garbage out.

I have been surprised by how many product teams are out of touch with why their users are using their software. Sometimes, a team tries to make a customer happy by giving them exactly what they want. Sometimes a vision from a leader in the company as to how *they* believe the world should be versus how it is without doing any market validation on the idea.

Misguided Why Case Study

At one software company I was brought in as CEO shortly after a private equity firm acquired them. The product team had started modernizing their product, but the feedback I received from sales was that the customers hated the design of the new product. The team had spent about one year designing the product and were in the early stages of starting to code it. There was a theory that the existing product was too complex. And that what the company needed was a software product that customers could sign up for themselves and use without any help or training.

The team also wanted to expand their market for the software and go after small and medium businesses. Therefore, the approach of customers signing up for software themselves was believed to be the answer. As a side note, this process is now called "product-led growth" in the software industry, and many products are sold this way. We will discuss this more later when discussing gGTM models. It is a great strategy and scales well, so I can understand why so many companies are drawn to this, including this software company.

But in this instance, it was not the right approach. The team showed me the old product and the new software. Yes, the old product was complex and packed a lot of information on the screens. The new design was very basic and removed 80% of the information that the prior product had on its screens, with no way to get the prior information anywhere in the new product. It was much simpler to use, but did it meet the needs of the end-users? Is this what customers wanted?

My next step was to speak with some of the existing customers. The company had been in existence for 18 years so there were plenty of customers to talk to who had a lot of experience with the software. My initial questions addressed why they used the software currently—what were their needs? They all had large inventories, a number of them had over one billion dollars in inventory. These customers were using the software to reduce this inventory without jeopardizing their business. For context, this inventory included spare parts needed to maintain the world's most critical infrastructure across the globe. I'm talking about industries that keep the lights on, mining operations, and oil and gas operations. As they put it, their "spending prior to the software had been out of control" and our software helped them make rapid decisions about how to adjust stock levels. For a good portion of their stock, they just trusted our software to make the right decision automatically. This was their "why."

However, asking why once is never enough, so I asked "why" they did not use their Enterprise Resource Planning (ERP) system to do this given these solutions manage inventory and companies spend a lot of money on ERP software. Then I asked "why" their inventories had grown so out of control in the first place. The answer was that their ERP system blindly generated replacement orders and did not optimize the stock levels because it did not consider all the correct information when making decisions. The ERP systems did not handle the complexity required to make a good decision. Their inventory had grown out of control. They were only able to review stock levels once every five years because the amount of staff they would need to hire to review the inventory using the old way would be in the hundreds! They could not afford to do that. These customers had far too few inventory planners compared to the millions of spare parts they would have to manage if they did not have our software.

Was I done yet? Of course not. I then asked "why" they used my company's software product to solve the problem. They answered that it gave them "all of the information they needed" in one place to make decisions faster and with greater accuracy. It also helped them focus on which parts to look at first. For less expensive parts they even let our software decide on its own so some of the work was automated.

So, what these companies were clearly saying was that they needed a user interface that gave them the detailed information needed for them to make quick decisions in a compact format and provide more automation. Sometimes a quick summary was not enough, therefore, they needed the ability to obtain even more data quickly. But sometimes it was enough, so having that quick snapshot screen was essential, using the 80/20 rule. The information the customers needed changed depending on what problem they were solving.

They also needed a way to further scale what they were doing which also screamed automation. I did not even need to ask them why they hated the new design for the software (but I did anyway, just to amuse myself). Of course, my next question was to my CTO, asking him, "why" the team was launching a product that dumbed down the user interface and was geared towards small and medium businesses?" It was to get into a new market but the company could not afford this move without additional funding. An obvious follow-up question was whether they had done any field testing on this new concept. The answer was an obvious "no."

The lack of understanding as to why customers were using the software in the first place allowed the product team to go down a wrong path fully convinced that customers needed a simpler user interface that obscured most of the information from them. They also believed that they could expand sales to a market segment that did not deal with the same level of complexity, did not have that many locations, and did not have millions of spare parts to manage. The existing customers and the customers in the new market segment already had this simpler user interface with their ERP system and it was not working. The screens in my albeit outdated software gave them everything they needed to make decisions—"why" they purchased my company's software in the first place. Take that away, and the product goes away.

Don't get me wrong, the screens in my product needed some major help as fields were added over time so the software had a user interface that looks like the team just kept adding fields as they went along, placing them in odd places. It was a reasonable conclusion that the user interface needed some work. However not understanding the "why" led the team off track with a user interface that removed all the necessary information from the screens, which was not what these customers needed. The conclusion: The product the team was building would tank the company's existing revenues and would go after an entirely different market. One that would require a lot of time and money to capture. If I did not modernize the company's existing software, I would lose our existing market and revenue, so we had to "pick a lane" as they say.

Software modernization can be expensive so I was worried we would not have the cash flow and resources to support that effort, let alone go after a new market. What I actually had was lumpy revenue that was driven by perpetual licenses, the majority of which came from one cyclical industry. I threw out the new design that this team had been working on for over a year, at first shocking the team. I then brought in a design team that understood what the customers needed and focused on the why.

So, where did this company end up? I am proud to say that we modernized the existing software and maintained a 99%+ retention rate throughout this transition. We also expanded into adjacent markets and geographies using the existing software. This is not always the case, but in this instance, entering new geographies and adjacent industries did not require new features in the software. The majority of the existing capabilities of the software worked for adjacent markets we had chosen, but in some instances, where some additional capabilities were needed, the new design was much more configurable and made it easier to support any of the additional requirements. The company was then sold to IBM, which has expanded the use of the software to many more companies across the globe.

Takeaways:

- Know "why" your software solution and company exists; without this clarity prioritization of features does not matter;
- Market pivots can be expensive so make sure you have adequate funding to make a drastic pivot before attempting it.
- It is ok to stop what you are doing, even if it means upsetting people who are over-invested in the current approach. Time already spent is a sunk cost.
- Success in managing products in a software company is not easily accomplished with a feature-led strategy. A more holistic approach is needed.

The Software Life Cycle

The software life cycle is often poorly understood and is the source of much-wasted money in the software industry. Comprehending the life cycle of a software product can save a significant sum of money. It applies to both single-product software companies and large software companies with broad product portfolios.

At one large software company, the finance organization would take the prior year's revenues from a software product, add 10-12%, and declare it as the sales forecast for the next year, regardless of where a software product was in its life cycle. This wasn't feasible because many of the company's software products were aging and were either in the "cash cow" phase or in decline. These phases should not all be treated the same.

The teams did not have much of a choice but to accept the forecast, all the while knowing that they had very little chance of hitting it. The numbers were deceiving because every few years, a product in decline could hit a quarter of growth when a large customer needed more licenses due to expanded use of the software within their company. Other times the customer had a software renewal of a subscription agreement that would temporarily increase the revenue. These examples are not growth per se, but a mismanaged process that commissioned sales reps for expansion and renewals. They were not closing new deals, and a financial forecasting process viewed an increase in bookings over the same quarter the prior year as growth.

What matters more is whether total revenues are increasing or decreasing. For this same company, the market obviously was not fooled by this as revenue declined for 24 straight quarters between 2015 and 2020. Coarse corrections were needed so I mapped the software for one of their portfolios to a diagram similar to the one below. I then asked the leadership team why software in the decline phase of the life cycle was expected to have a 10% growth target? It certainly helped set more realistic targets going forward. Although old habits die hard in a large company with high pressure for growth. Using a life-cycle approach led to many productive discussions about which products should be sent through the re-invest cycle, if any.

Let's discuss the software life cycle in more detail to avoid these types of mistakes. Not all software is the same but a good majority of software in today's market has six major phases within its life cycle;

- Ideation
- Launch
- Growth
- Cash cow
- Decline
- Re-invest

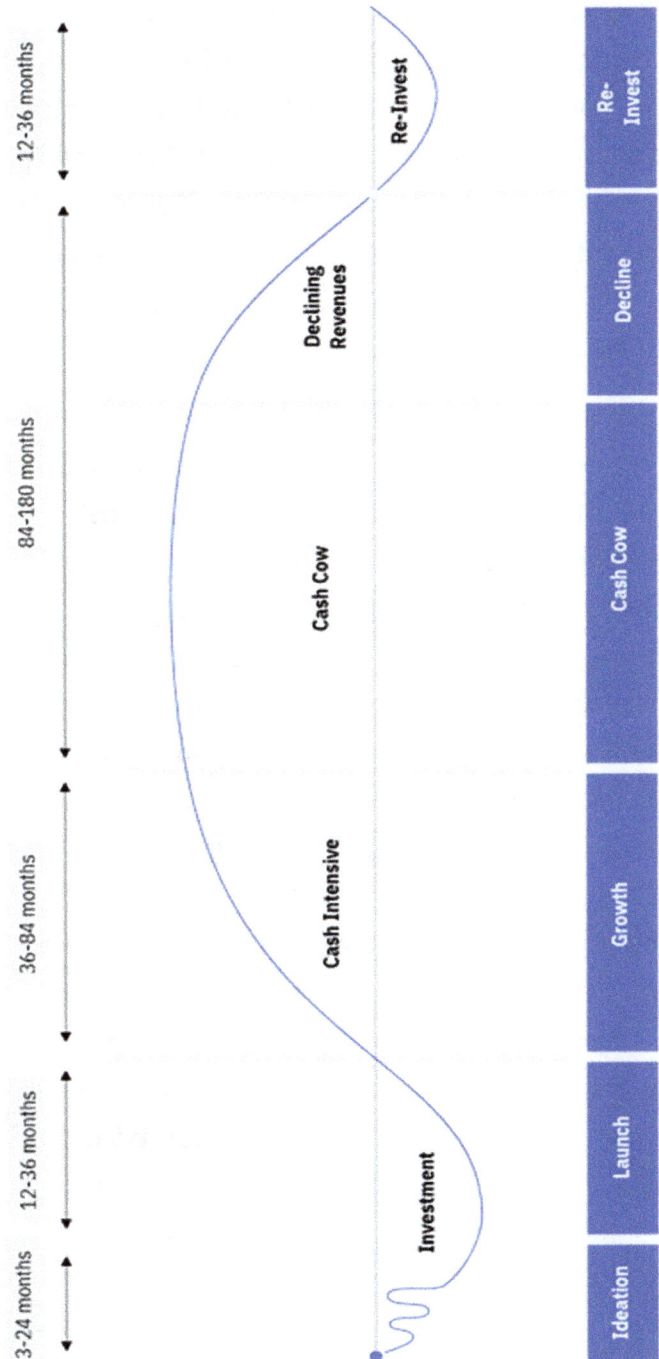

The timeframes in the diagram above can and will vary depending on how quickly innovation is occurring in your market, especially with consumer-oriented software; so adjust accordingly. The time frames on the diagram are where most enterprise software sits and is how I have been launching software products.

Ideation

This is the research phase of the product, where it may not be 100% clear that there is a product or a market behind an idea. This is one of the most challenging phases of a new product launch, especially when innovation is involved. You can say that user research can help in this area, but did anyone ever say they needed to send out strings of 128 bytes of data (Twitter until recently), or did anyone express wanting to share what they ate for breakfast online (Facebook) or that they desired a phone without a keypad (iPhone)? One could even argue that a handheld computer had already been tried and failed (Apple Newton). At some point during the ideation phase, you have to "pick a lane" and then ideally prototype, even if just on paper, exactly what the product will include. With the right design team, this can be accomplished quickly.

Launch

This is my favorite phase. During this phase, product market fit is defined, the product features and functions are mapped out, and the product is built. For most software, this phase requires a capital injection as there are very few software products that can be built without investment. Software developers and the infrastructure to run the software are expensive. Early adopter customers are sought out and issues with the software are worked out during this phase to eventually scale the business. During this phase, pivoting or changing direction is more likely to occur as the market can be dynamic and interactions with customers convince the team there may be more significant opportunities. A product launch is not for the faint of heart. Many in the software industry never experience this process, as most individuals join during the growth phase. I equate the launch process to running a marathon. It is a long hard run, and you just don't stop until you get to the finish line.

Growth

Software can enter the growth phase once a critical mass of features are built to add enough value to a product that customers are willing to write a check to obtain the software. This is when you pour gas on the fire if there is a large market for the software. The growth phase is the most dynamic and fun part of the life cycle as new employees are hired, product investments are made, and new customers are onboarded. Managing profitability in this phase becomes critical, although some companies sacrifice profitability to capture market share. Uber and Amazon, for example, lost money for years on end before becoming profitable. Ideally, your software has been translated so overall growth also includes global expansion. It is surprising how many software companies miss the opportunity to expand globally. I remind those people that the way you make money in software is to build it once and then sell it over-and-over again. Seems obvious, no?

Cash Cow

A cash cow product is a beautiful thing if properly managed. By definition, a cash cow product requires less money to maintain than it produces. It usually has been in the market for a long time and has a full feature set, so the product requires little investment unless it is aging and needs to be modernized. A typical state for this phase is that little to no new customers are being added but that many of the existing customers are sticking around. These products can produce large amounts of cash if managed properly. I have leveraged cash cow products to fund the reinvestment cycle for the cash cow product as well as ancillary products in a portfolio. The common mistake during this cycle is not optimizing operations so that the product generates large amounts of cash. This is often because the company is in denial, thinking there must be something wrong with the sales team, and if they could only fix them, the sales would start to increase again—not true. Your product is old and out of date.

Beyond that common misconception, I also caution against significant investment in features. These are also a waste of resources unless there is additional market share to capture or the company is truly planning to modernize the product and send it into a re-invest cycle. There are many examples of mature software solutions where so many features have been added that the users do not understand nor use over 80% of them. Having spent a significant amount of time at start-ups, I have used this fact against larger more mature products, classifying them as old, difficult to learn and to use. For example, I am a huge fan of Microsoft Excel, but I see many in the younger generations adopting solutions like Google Sheets due to its simplicity.

Changing the mindset towards streamlining the business is a game changer for most cash cow products. Price increases, if properly managed, can be used to increase the cash being generated. Investments in optimizing infrastructure can make sense. Reducing feature development to focus more on product stability can be helpful for end users. Automating the routine tasks associated with running the software is essential and will help your team scale operations better.

A smart move in this phase is to focus on user groups to help make the software more "sticky." This references convincing customers to expand usage and to stick around longer. Attending to the needs of your existing customers also helps fight off competitors who may be entering the market with newer, more modern offerings. Sending out information to the install base (current customers) on how to use a feature of the software they have not yet tried would be wise, given the goal of this phase is to extend the life cycle as much as possible. In addition, the employees within the software company oftentimes have long-standing relationships with some of these customers, so maintaining these connections as you are streamlining operations is critical to avoid losing your base (stickiness). You may have to re-think your organizational structure as you make this transition.

Decline

Unfortunately, all good things come to an end. Most software products start to decline in years seven to ten because newer technologies make the software look old and outdated. In some markets, decline can happen even sooner. As revenues decline, the cost of maintaining the software can be higher than the revenues coming from the software. Sometimes a company might retreat to a position of only providing critical bug fixes or security patches. Customers are usually aware that the software is in decline, but the cost of replacing it is high, or they have other higher proprietary problems to address in their business, so they are just looking to maintain the status quo.

Re-Invest

Sometimes, it makes sense to make a significant investment in a software product with a large install base to modernize it. I did this with IBM Maximo, a software product that had at that time a 30-year life cycle, with one or possibly two prior re-invest cycles, depending upon who you asked. The install base is the closest thing I have ever seen to a software cult that loves the solution. I had never seen anything like it and I felt I had the responsibility (or burden) to preserve it.

Modernization includes updating both the front end and architecture of the software. I have to say this because it is often believed that updating just the user interface is good enough. It is not enough. The software industry continually changes, and the latest innovations include hybrid and AI-enabled software. Whereas, the prior adaptation was software as a service and before that, client-server software. By the time I write this book, there possibly will be the next iteration of what is considered modern software architecture. So, imagine putting a new user interface on a client-server application and then watching your business get decimated by SaaS companies who convinced large companies to move away from running their data centers. There is so much to be said about how to modernize a product (and how not to) that an entire book could be written on it.

By now, you should have an idea of where your product sits on in its lifecycle. I would suggest you go one step further and map out the entire life cycle of your product. It should not take that long and it's well worth it. You may have some portions of the software in one life cycle and others in another. To start, address these questions:

- Are you expecting your solution to have a three-year, five-year or even a fifteen-year life cycle?
- Why do you believe what you believe about your software's entire life cycle?
- What are some yet to occur scenarios that "could" disrupt its life cycle?
- How likely are those scenarios to happen?

One of my favorite books that helped me look into the future was written by Annie Duke called, *Thinking in Bets: Making Smarter Decisions When You Do Not Have All the Facts* (Duke, 2018). Annie Duke is a world-famous poker player who has taken her approach to winning in poker to business leaders. She recognized that, like a poker player, business decisions are often made without having all the information necessary to make the right decision, 100% of the time.

What did I learn from her book? Well, my thought process now includes assigning probabilities to certain scenarios succeeding or certain events happening, and creating a decision tree based on those statistics. I also take a hard look at each of the potential bets I can make and look to find the flaws in each one of them. Then, I admit to where I may have bias. For example, where am I assigning a high probability to a bet just because I am more familiar with it and, therefore, am biased towards that approach? Am I truly listening to what my investors, employees, and customers are saying?

I am not advocating gambling, but in the business world, you have to map out your bets and then take one or you will be left behind. So as a leader I ask myself "Am I getting my team to do something they would not have otherwise done on their own?" The reality is that the majority of your team will chug along without you doing a single thing or making a single decision. Therefore, when mapping out a strategy for your product, it is your responsibility to help yourself or your team think through the actions that are necessary to help your company grow.

Takeaways:

- Understand where in the product life cycle your product exists.
- Map out a course for your product's entire life cycle.
- Make clear decisions about the structure of your team and go-to-market based on where you are at in the software life cycle.
- Invest in the right talent to bring your product through a re-investing life cycle.
- Map out the lifecycle of your software and the varying bets you and your company could take.
- Make a bet. Do not sit still.

Artifacts:

Download The Software Life Cycle Diagram

Messaging

The biggest mistake I see companies make is in their messaging. Trying to understand what they do from their website is like a Sherlock Holmes murder mystery where they murdered their message, and it is a mystery as to what their company does. Out of all the things a software company has to do, messaging is one of the most difficult. Proper time and attention need to be spent on messaging and the CEO, Head of Product, sales, and marketing need to be directly involved. This is not something you delegate. Why? Simply because the best messaging often wins, not the best product.

> **You heard me correctly, in software, messaging is that important.**

I can give you numerous examples. If you are old enough to have been around for the early days of Microsoft Windows, you will remember that Windows 3.0 was a pixelated mess. It looked like a bad video game of the Pong Era (apologies in advance if you worked on this!) The graphical operating systems running on Unix workstations and the early Apple Macintosh were much better. Apple, for one, used vector-based graphics so the screens rendered extremely fast. The fonts were modeled after calligraphy, and the usability of the entire system was very intuitive. One could learn how to use a Mac by just sitting in front of it for a little while. Windows was also so "buggy" that the error screen obtained the name "the blue screen of death." So why did Microsoft win? They were selling to the Chief Information Officers of large companies, and their focus was providing an operating system with the right software to operate a business. After winning over the CIO, when individuals had to use a Windows PC at work, they then wanted the same type of computer at home. I was annoyed by this, given the Mac was a much better computer that did not crash as often. Unfortunately, back then, Mac computers were large and bulky so they were not easily moved. Even I gave in and purchased a PC!

Apple, on the other hand, had a reputation for Steve Jobs calling CIOs vulgar names because he saw them as a bottleneck for getting anything done at large companies (Elmer, 2014). I sometimes feel his pain, but restraint is important. He also knew he had the best product and that everyone should just recognize this. History has shown that he both learned and became the best in the industry at messaging as a result of this mistake early in his career.

Hopefully, you are now convinced that messaging is important. So, what should you do next? Let's start with some rules to follow as you define your messaging.

Keep it simple. A customer should be able to repeat the message after only hearing it once.

- Be different. I launched a product in the supply chain space and at a large conference there were no less than 10 booths that had the same messaging. What a disaster for those companies.

- Avoid being cute or clever. As tempting as it is, these messages rarely go over well. If I am trying to get a customer to write a big check for a product and have to explain to their CFO that spending 1 million dollars on "your clever company name" just makes the sale more difficult. If anything goes wrong, the buyer may be worried about the perception of others who may say, "What did you expect by buying software from "clever company name?" There is always an exception, but good luck with that. Kudos to "Dude Solutions," acquired by Siemens in 2022 as they were a rare exception to this rule.

- Invoke emotion with your messaging. This is not always achievable with all products. Amazon did a great job of messaging its "1-click" purchase option as they addressed the deep frustration (and possibly anger) of many online buyers trying to navigate shopping websites. This was in the early days of online shopping, before technology became more robust.

- Tell a story. They are more likely to be remembered. Before books, people told stories to pass down information to the next generation. One way to tell a story is to ask a question. For example, "Do you really want someone with an inferior product but much, much better messaging to beat you in the market?" There are some great resources on storytelling. Pixar, whose entire business is built upon storytelling, has a master class on storytelling that can put you in a storytelling frame of mind.

Once you create your hypothesis for what messaging the team believes will work, a first meeting sales deck known as a "level one" deck should be created and tested with some initial customers. It is called a level one deck because it is the first presentation with the customer. Can you guess what the second meeting deck is called? Your level one deck will take a few iterations (See the section on creating a level one deck). After a few meetings, you will know if your messaging is working or not. Typically, what I am looking for are customers jumping out of their seats excited about the discussion they just had with you and are already discussing how to proceed. This is the power of messaging. It could take some time and several iterations to get customers excitedly engaged, but it's worth the effort. Some companies never get there.

Messaging In Practice

At the Servigistics company, the marketing team led a process to revamp the messaging. The goal was to create a new category and then own that category because no one would have the solution besides Servigistics, of course. The end result was a new category called Strategic Service Management (SSM) and a new role in a company called the Chief Service Officer. The creation of a new category was brilliant. Servigistics immediately became the leader in this new category (given they created it). For years, no one even came close to the lead that Servigisitcs maintained in the SSM category. The category name was also easy to remember. It put their software on par with ERP, SCM, CRM and other 3-letter VIP acronyms being thrown around in the industry. Analysts wrote white papers on Strategic Service Management, further fueling the category. The final "oh my gosh" moment is when companies started naming executives the Chief Service Officer. It makes sense and is an important role in a company where great service is required to maintain customers. Interestingly enough, another set of companies, seven plus years later, hijacked CSO and declared it to be the Chief Security Officer to capitalize on the growing cyber security software market.

Takeaway:

- The best messaging wins in the end, not always the best product.

Artifact:

Download The Software Messaging Guide

Talent

My perspective on talent has changed drastically over the years. Early in my career, I was looking to find and hire the smartest people possible. I then learned that some of the smart people I hired, despite being intelligent, were not capable of working within a team and some did not have a strong work ethic. They were applying their intelligence and creativity towards getting out of doing work. So, my hiring mantra became "smart and gets things done." I did not coin this term. I first heard this term from Joel Spolsky who has a book by the same name, which perfectly describes my style. Although now a bit dated, *Smart and Gets Things Done* (Spolsky, 2007) is a great book that first convinced me to find and hire the best technical talent and to be intentional as to how you do it.

> **Every single position in your company counts, especially in a startup.**

Talent is so critical I would say it is more important than 50% of the other areas mentioned in this book.

Great companies find and retain the best individuals they can find, anywhere in the world. Trying to operate a company with the wrong team was a hard lesson for me to learn. It is certainly easier to be tolerant of "good enough" or sometimes I had the notion that it was quicker to just "do it myself." Unfortunately, neither scales well because building software is a team sport and everyone must be on their game. Managing talent is so vital that as a leader, my goal is to spend 50% of time either finding new/better talent or investing my time in the people who already work for me.

Someone I worked with on a successful project where radical change was needed, recently scheduled time with me to ask for advice on how to transform her new team. One of the questions she had was, "What do you do with the people who don't want to go along with the new direction?" I am always willing to hear anyone out. Some of my best employees challenge ideas knowing that I am always willing to listen. However, what she was asking about was a very different situation than an employee with good intentions trying to give input. She needed to know: What if someone is unwilling to adapt to the needed direction? It was a good question. The way I would answer it now is very different from how I mistakenly answered it earlier in my career. Early on, I would spend an inordinate amount of time trying to bring these skeptical individuals along. Now I know somewhere between one to ten percent of people will never see things your way. I have learned to move these individuals off the team or out of the organization early on if the area they disagree with is critical to your success. It is unhealthy for both you and them to continue forward if you ultimately disagree with the direction. I do, however, have one rule when doing this. No one should ever be surprised if you move them off the team. Always give the employee a chance to work toward the direction you are setting and as a team player. Ask yourself if you are putting in a lot of effort to help bring someone else along, but no matter how much prodding you do, they are just not as committed to the cause as you are. You can give it your best effort, but at some point, you and the team need to move on.

Ideally, I want 9 out of 10 hires to hit the mark. No one is perfect at hiring and there is no way to learn everything about someone before you hire them. Once you work with someone you learn much more about their work habits and capabilities. Given that I know that possibly one in ten are not going to be a fit, I always build into my plans a way to smoothly transition them out of the business. The majority of the one out of ten in my experience manage themselves out of the business.

For example, if working collaboratively is a huge part of the culture and an individual is looking to be the rock star that everyone admires and the world revolves around, they will learn very quickly that a team-based organization is not a good fit for them. They will be running counterculture to the rest of the team. For individuals who do not fit the "and gets things done" profile, the transparency in my approach makes it obvious they are not getting much done compared to their peers. Each week, even at the executive level, my direct reports show up to a team call with a 1-page slide where they have:

- Discussion points
- Accomplishments prior week
- Plan for this week (current week)
- Issues (for the team to resolve)
- Decide (decisions that need to be made)

- Remind (items someone on the team was supposed to do)

During the team call each person presents their slide and mainly discusses the items under discussion points. Although it becomes tedious to hear someone go through their accomplishments and plan for the week item by item (we can all read!), this creates the ultimate transparency and helps both me and my team ensure we are all on the same page and aware of what each person is doing. This includes me. I want my team to keep me accountable. As the saying goes, iron sharpens iron."

I subsequently also require all managers to meet with their employees once a week. We use the same 1-1 template as we do for the team standup, just updated with topics that are more appropriate for 1:1 conversations between a manager and the employee. I had a manager once who did not call me for two months. I finally scheduled some time with him and he started the meeting by asking "if something was the matter." Nothing was the matter except that he was not actually being a manager. Maybe he recognized I was completely unmanageable and gave up.

Most people take feedback and can course correct, but there is a segment of the population where course correction comes only after you fire them, or after the next person at the next company they work at fires them. Then there is an even smaller percentage where course correction never happens. I can say that one of the biggest mistakes I made early in my career is not dealing with misaligned talent quickly enough. Both the individual who was possibly in a position to fail, as well as the organization, suffered as a result of my indecision to take action quickly enough.

Not all talent issues are fixed by letting someone go. As stated, my personal goal is to spend at least 50% of my time investing in the talent in the company. This not only includes finding talent, it also includes the people who already work for me. I want everyone to walk away from having worked with me or my team as a better resource and possibly even a better person outside of work. I also expect them to make me a better person as a result of this investment of time that involves both of us.

I speak from experience. The time spent investing in others has paid off for me because I learned while making investments in them. Working at a large company where I was blocked from hiring the correct talent for much of the four years I was there forced me to take existing talent and train them. This was good for me as it challenged me to take a step back and rethink how to quickly upskill existing talent given that hiring the right people was off the table. The individuals in this large company were smart and eager to learn quickly so this made investing time in them easier. The content of this book was partly produced because of this effort. Upskilling existing talent certainly burned a lot more time, but over time I scaled my efforts. For example, I learned that I could cross-pollinate one skill set on one team and then use the individuals on this team to cross-pollinate this skill to all the other teams. I intentionally only focused on one area with each team as it allowed them to really hone in and become best-in-class for whatever area I had them focus on.

Note that the approach of cross-pollination only works when you have a large number of teams to draw upon and have both the time and money to make this type of investment. At a smaller startup, every person counts, and you cannot afford to have even a single person on the team who is not performing. For example, many start-ups have only a single marketing person. If they are not performing, the inbound sales lead funnel can, and will be broken, affecting the company's sales.

The worst-case scenario is the "toxic employee." This individual slows down the entire team and seems to always go left when the entire team wants to go right. I have sometimes joked that this individual has been planted in my company by one of my competitors. They are easy to spot as they did their fair share of contributing to the issues the company was facing.

Toxic employees need to be moved out of the company quickly. Every company I have come to transform has had at least one toxic employee. The worst instance of a toxic employee was in a company I had taken over as CEO in which there was a sales rep who would get in people's faces and yell at them. In my first week as CEO, he sat in my office for 45 minutes and told me every wrong the company had committed for the past 10 years. The entire floor heard him yelling at me through my closed door. I could have easily ended the conversation, but it was interesting to hear the background of the company and how he believed he had been wronged. He told me his office during one period of the company's history was in the utility closet. After that, I could not get the movie *Office Space* (Judge, 1999) out of my head.

I asked him a few questions along the way and at the end of his rant he thanked me and equated me to a therapist, stating that he felt much better after speaking with me. I had no intention of being his therapist given I had an entire company to run and no credentials in providing actual therapy. When I told the head of HR that I was going to let this individual go, they were concerned that he would "go postal" and show up at the office with a weapon or do something drastic. I was not concerned but to make everyone happy I decided to meet this individual offsite. It is always a good practice to have at least one other person from the company with you as a witness, so I brought along the Chairman of the Board. This toxic employee was of course late. I looked over at the chairman and he was sweating. He admitted he was nervous and then asked me, "Aren't you nervous?" I responded very seriously by saying "not really, I can definitely outrun you. So, I'm all good." He looked shocked before he realized I was joking as I started to chuckle (although I could outrun him).

The individual finally turned up, and we had a cordial conversation where he stated that he was impressed that someone in the company finally had the backbone to let him go. It turns out, he knew all along that his behavior was inappropriate and that he was not doing any real meaningful work. I had met with him a few times to review his work and those reviews did not go well; he had a hard time explaining exactly what he had been doing.

Early on, I did not deal with toxic employees quickly enough and regretted it as the company suffered as a result. I would let things drag on, sometimes for months on end. Did I really want the hassle of finding someone else? Can't I just fix this person who is ruining my business? This becomes even more difficult when they are doing some things right, but other critical items the wrong way.

Removing the toxic employee I described above had a good outcome for everyone involved and fortunately no one went postal on me. Even though it was by far the most difficult employee situation I had encountered to date as a leader, you must do the hard stuff, not just occupy the seat. I strongly believe there are two types of executives, "sitters" and those who "get things done." A sitter sits in their chair, collects a big salary and has a big title, but does not do the hard stuff. I had numerous employees thank me for removing this employee from the business. He did change his mind later and tried to sue me, but he missed the filing deadline in Texas by one day. For once I was glad he was a slacker.

So, where did I get my ideas to change how I dealt with my employees, toxic or otherwise? Honestly, I learned how to better manage team dynamics and deal with toxic employees by watching every episode of *The Apprentice*. This was long before Donald Trump became a politically charged household name. It did not matter to me who the host of the show was, I was interested in the psychology behind teams. This was the perfect learning ground. You had two teams. One would raise 100k for charity and the other would raise 10k? Why such different results? They both started with the same number of resources. Each team had the same number of people, time, and level of funding (zero). If you have seen the show, you will notice a trend where on the losing teams there seems to always be *that* person who wants to go one way while the rest of the team wants to go another. They wind up burning the team's precious time, energy, and sometimes their will to succeed. So I knew I did not need or want that person on my team.

Employment Agreements

I am not giving legal advice and would advise you instead to find a good employment lawyer and an IP lawyer at your disposal. Need convincing? Well, since you are at a software company you will need an employment agreement signed by each employee that ensures you own any intellectual property that is created while they are employed by your company. You will also want the agreement to cover both non-compete and non-solicitation. The software industry is ripe with examples of competitors stealing employees, creating a competing company, or taking IP with them out the door. I was out of town when an employee was let go. When I got back I asked one of my managers "How did it go?" She looked at me a bit puzzled and said he took a "really long time packing his desk." Of course, I had to ask "how long?" She responded by saying "almost two hours." This puzzled me for a couple of days when I applied the "if it does not make sense, what information am I missing" rule. What was I missing? Well, I asked our IT lead to look at his computer logs. Sure enough, he was copying the entire code base to a cloud drive and was waiting for it to finish. Bingo. Ok, you say, "Not every employee is going to try and steal your code base!" What if a competitor simply hires an employee who is privy to the direction of your software? Employee laws vary by state so you will want to ensure that you have an employment lawyer review your agreement for every state and country from which you hire employees. This seems daunting but it is typically only a few hours per state/country.

Takeaways:

- Adopt the "Smart and Get Thing Done" model.
- Remove toxic employees, you will do both you and the toxic individual a favor.
- Invest in upskilling your team members. It will pay dividends for both the individuals and you.
- Because you are managing intellectual property, put employment agreements in place, even with founders.
- Self-reflect: Are you getting things done or are you sitting in the position with the title not making the hard decisions needed to move your business forward? Do not take it personally as I have had to ask myself this question.

Artifacts:

Download Talent Matrix

Culture

Culture is one of the most difficult areas to get correct. You may be dealing with a team and an organization that has been doing things the same way for a long time. Coming in with a new approach is not always welcome. As I was transitioning a large organization to my approach I had plenty of detractors. But I kept them so busy transforming the way they were working and did it at such a rapid pace, I am pretty sure they did not have much time to stop and complain. I would sometimes even "leak" the changes because gossiping across teams was rampant in this company, so I used it to my advantage as an informal way to adopt change. The teams were sometimes so proud they "knew ahead of time" what was coming that they forgot to get upset or worry about the actual change.

This was all intentional.

I also did not spend a lot of time learning how things worked before joining the organization. I knew the approach I used to generate better results and because I had an idea of the existing output of the teams I knew where they stood. I also knew if I was incorrect, I would get immediate feedback from any team that had a better methhod. It was just a faster approach to get to the same place than spending months of analysis on current processes.

My approach to identifying my own self-bias came in handy here.

Every situation and team is unique and there is no one size fits all culture. You have to tailor it based on both your personality and that of the team/company. Because of this, I can only give you some ideas on how to define the right culture for your team. Here are some of the culture bullet points I utilize with my teams (to get you started):

1. **Smart and gets things done (Spolsky, 2007).** This is the overriding culture among all other things. This phrase sets the tone for how we work as a team and that we are going to be a team made up of high achievers.

2. **Be team-oriented.** There is no "smartest person" in the room on my team. Part of getting things done is bringing the team along with you and knowing when to let go of your personal ego to do the best for the company. It is ok and even encouraged to debate ideas, but once a decision has been made, a healthy team moves forward as a team. Once a direction has been set, you have to be "all in." Undermining the team because you do not 100% agree with the approach is unacceptable. If you often do not agree with your team, it is possible that you are on the wrong team, not necessarily an issue with the team. No team agrees 100% of the time.

3. **Foster innovation and creativity.** Innovation can happen at all levels within a company. Celebrate innovative ideas and creativity and it will grow organically. The most significant gains in innovation are when a team takes existing ideas and puts them together in a new and unique way. The reason for this is that it builds upon pre-existing work. Too often in software development a creative approach means entirely throwing away the existing to create the new. An example of that would be iTunes (now called Apple Music but will forever be called iTunes in my mind). There were already several MP3 players in existence, music download sites (Naptster) and e-commerce sites to acquire and listen to your favorite music. What Apple did was combine all three of these attributes into a single device that was simple to use and made it extremely easy to purchase and download new songs from an e-commerce store. The combination of these three items in a new and creative manner forever changed the music, online music content, and MP3 industries.

4. **Operate with transparency.** Do this if you want to gain the trust of your team, customers, and stakeholders. With the exception of HR-related information that is protected by law and financials if the company is publicly traded,

the team is transparent about everything. As a CEO, my employees would have been surprised by how much I knew about what was going on at all times. No other person talks to the entire cross-section of employees, partners, customers, or vendors as often as the CEO. It is the cross-section of all these functions that allows you to piece together what is really going on in your company and make those critical decisions.

5. **Eliminate blockers**. A typical blocker in most organizations is the inability to pick up the phone and call the person you need to speak with. Sometimes this happens because a hierarchical organizational structure has been ingrained into the culture for a long time. The problem is when you want to include someone in your meeting but to do so, you have to then include their manager. Meetings then become exponentially bloated when everyone's manager is on a call when the intention was to just make them aware of the call. From my perspective, in even the largest organization, anyone should be able to pick up the phone and talk to whoever they need to in the company. Certainly, train people to use good judgment. Some suggestions to follow:

   a. If you are going to call the CEO and complain about something, you have the ability to do so, but you also do so at your peril (or maybe benefit).

b. Managers should use good judgment. For example, one good rule is that if someone has an issue with another employee and has not spoken with that individual first, then the manager needs to send that person back to work it out first before taking it up the chain (with the exception being a sensitive HR issue which should always be reported immediately).

c. Managers should meet with their employees one-on-one weekly and be transparent about what they are doing (see 1:1 template in prior chapter). This approach eliminates the need to meet with three layers of managers to get to the resource you "really" need to speak with. Everyone is operating with transparency and therefore, does not need to be copied on everything. Certainly, if another manager is using all of your team's time and you need them focused on something else, then you, as a manager, must intervene and work it out yourself. The reality is that this is more of an exception than the norm. So I don't suggest building a hierarchy where you have to gain approval to speak with someone because it causes a level of inefficiency.

6. **Be customer-oriented**. Be fanatical about driving real value to your customers. Being honest with yourself about what is adding value to your customers and what is nice to have is important.

7. **Be people-oriented**. Invest in your people and treat them with respect. Investments in the people on your team will deliver exponential long-term benefits. You decide what this looks like for your company. Is it training? Time? Stock? Cash compensation? Treating people with respect is a given.

8. **Be investor-oriented**. Realize that investors have put money into your company and expect a return, so meeting their expectations is essential. If you do not like that, become an investor.

(Note for 6-8, the single person who needs to balance 6,7,8 is the CEO. It is a tricky position to be in as sometimes when one area wins, the other loses. All three have to be balanced to be a healthy company.)

9. **Be purpose-driven**. As a company, you should have a purpose for existing. Whatever that may be. Once again, this needs to be tailor-fit to your company. On one of my teams, we were eliminating millions of miles of drive time by optimizing the routes of field service technicians. Our software made a difference. We also did charity work together as a team. One week,

instead of going out to eat on our regular team lunch, we made 100's of sack lunches consisting of PB&J sandwiches and went around town and handed them out to homeless people.

10. **Be a village**. It takes a village to change the world. Work well with others outside your company to deliver even greater value to your customers. All too often competitors are seen as the enemy instead of a potential partner. The CEO of Microsoft, Satya Nadella, shortly after taking over as CEO, pivoted the company's strategy to see Apple as both a partner, customer, and competitor at the same time. This new perspective allowed Microsoft to ship Office onto the iPhone sooner, which then led to a collaboration that delivered the Office Suite onto the iPad faster (Hit Refresh, Nadella et al. 2017). The prior approach could have resulted in Apple choosing a different company such as Google G Suite to be the productivity software of choice for the iPad.

Take-Aways:

- Be intentional when it comes to culture.
- Define your culture. Write it down on paper.
- Challenge the culture, and adjust, when appropriate.

Artifacts:

Download The Software Culture Guide

DESIGN, DEVELOPMENT AND PRODUCT

Ask anyone who has worked in the design, development and product organizations in the software industry and you will get an earful on what they have seen done wrong. Before diving into product, design and development execution I want to mention the top three most common mistakes I have seen in software. They are as follows:

- Focusing only on the 'product' versus the team and process that delivers the product
- Not being "all-in" with Agile
- Lack of discipline concerning requirements

Let's first go through each one of these to set the context for a more detailed discussion on product, design, and software development.

Building the Machine

You can spend 100% of your time on the product itself and if you do not build the flywheel that keeps it running things will deteriorate quickly. A favorite quote from Elon Musk is, "Create the machine that creates the machine." This requires a maniacal focus on finding the best talent, building the culture, processes, and having the best product strategy. A product, development, and design team that is a true product machine is fun to both be a part of and to watch. It is easy to recognize because you will see progress week over week (quarter over quarter) and even have surprises along the way where someone on the team delivers something unexpected and over the top innovative. Start with getting a smaller, more efficient product machine running first. About 75% of the software products I have launched were done with less than 10 people. Many of them stayed that size or only grew to teams of 20 people or less. This smaller team size does not mean that the software or problem we delivered was small. These small teams created big products, oftentimes, competing against competitors with 10x the amount of funding and resources than we had.

The machine, once built, needs to then have a mission. More of a personal story is that my little sister called me (a long time ago) to tell me she was getting married. Being younger myself, and less poised, I asked her a couple of questions because I knew the guy she was dating and I did not like him. The first question was, "Do you have a ring?" To this she answered "No, not yet." Then I asked her, "Do you have a date for this wedding?" Uncomfortably, she also answered "no" to this question. I then exclaimed, "Well then! You are not getting married." You see, you need a ring and a date (derived from Scrum: The Art of Doing Twice the Work in Half the Time, Sutherland & Sutherland, 2014). The same is true with software products. Nothing happens without a committed team and a date or event to rally the team around; just like my sister without a ring or a date thankfully never married that guy. The dates should be aggressive but not a death march (Death March, Yourdon, 1997). In the following chapter on product, design and development, I will describe how to create a product machine and manage the delivery incrementally to ensure the overall timeline is met. Speaking of timelines, let's discuss Agile.

"All In" Agile

The machine I just described is powered by a product delivery process, and in my case, my preferred approach is to combine the best of Agile with Scrum. For those unfamiliar with Agile or Scrum, they are project management methodologies, breaking project objectives into specific phases with an emphasis on teamwork and continuous improvement. My goal here is to not provide a primer on Agile or Scrum best practices as there are plenty of books on that. Give Scrum: Doing Twice the Work in Half the Time (Sutherland & Sutherland, 2014) a read if you need more information. I am only going to discuss the most common and largest mistake I have seen in incorrectly adopting the process which I describe as being "all in" on Agile, like the song by Lifehouse.

On my first day as Head of Product at a large software company, I wanted to set the stage for what is important to me. I told the teams that we would be using Agile. The company's senior leadership had set up a centralized team of resources who were Agile coaches to help teams adopt the practice; for once I did not seem to be going against the grain. As I met with team after team, they all said they were using Agile. I asked them all to send me their latest burn down. A burndown is an Agile chart depicting work completed as compared to the work left to be completed. It looks like a right triangle sloping downwards if work is being completed. If scope changes occur mid-stream, the chart looks like a mountain range with spikes designating where the scope was increased.

This should not have been a difficult request to fulfill but something unusual happened. They all asked if they could get back to me in a couple of weeks. This was odd as a team using Agile should have at least the burndown from their last sprint. Sprints are a list of work to be completed, by whom, how long each task is planned to take, and during what period of time (e.g. over the next 2 weeks). At the end of any sprint, the work gets reviewed, and a burndown should be produced to show the progression.

At that time, I had about 125 product managers and many distinct products within my scope. I had a wide variety of teams, but they all pretty much said the same thing. Let me get back to you. Huh? When I dug in deeper it turned out that the development team was using Agile sprint planning, but the product and design teams were not included in the Agile process. The marketing team was using Agile, but no one outside of their organization knew as the product teams had not been included in their marketing-specific Agile process. When I asked them to share their sprint plan with me they initially refused. Product pages would change and the product team had no idea it was happening. They looked uninformed in front of sales and customers asking questions about the product using information they obtained on the website.

Thankfully, the Agile coaches turned out to be invaluable. Because I was in a larger company and I was new to the organization, the team members were not always comfortable being transparent about what was going on. However, the individuals who met with the Agile coaches one on one were. The coaches were reporting back to me that team members were asking questions such as, "What is a burndown? I have no idea what he is asking for!"

It turns out that this is a pretty common issue. The majority of the products I was assigned at this large software company had come into the company via acquisition. The teams from the acquired companies were using the methodology they had when the company had acquired them. This was not unique to this particular software company either. The previous software companies I had worked for as CEO all had the exact same issue. How can so many companies get this wrong?

So, how should Agile be implemented? For a product, Agile involves having the product, design, and development teams all on a single burndown; it's an all-around collaboration. Again, a burndown is a chart that shows completed work compared to planned work over the expected timeframe sloping down as work is completed. If no work is completed it flatlines like a dead person's heart monitor. Each team's completed sprints are usually 2 weeks long work phases. For mature or more complex products, sprints may be as long as 3-4 weeks in duration. A burndown list includes who on the team is doing what during the sprint and in what order. The sprint therefore, is the grouping of all of the items on the list into a timeframe. The actual burndown is updated at least once a week. Some of the tools out there such as Jira keep it continuously up to date.

There is typically a weekly sprint playback meeting that shows the progress that has been made. In the playback, the burndown is displayed showing a list of items completed and then the list of remaining items to be completed in the sprint. The playback meetings usually include participants from the development, product, and design teams.

I typically run a separate but parallel burndown for GTM activities. This integrates sales, sales enablement, presales, marketing, and product into a single burndown. I typically tell the product owner for the product burndown to attend the GTM burndown meetings and visa versa. Actually, anyone who attends either burndown is welcome to listen in. But you're probably asking why I split the go-to-market activities from the regular cadence of producing the product? It is because software developers typically do not want to sit in a meeting and listen to details regarding a digital marketing campaign, a sales play, or a discussion on improvements being made to the customer sales deck. So when the burndowns are split out of practicality there becomes a point in which there is no incremental benefit to providing additional transparency to a team or individual; in this instance, most just want to get their coding done and not sit in meetings all day.

Each burndown has a clear product owner. Think of that person as the quarterback for the sprint. The product owner can change from sprint to sprint, although, most of the time it does not. All participants have clarity as to what they are supposed to be doing. Items that are not on the burndown are not completed; they are put onto the next sprint. There are always exceptions, but they should be rare and should get approved via a triage process. Yes, like in a hospital, triage is the practice of determining which tasks are most critical and need to be addressed first; it's prioritization.

Then there are always questions about what follow-up meetings are needed. The goal is to have as few meetings as possible with as few people as possible because work does not get done in meetings. Each week, the product owner runs a backlog grooming call where the product owner prioritizes items in the sprint and reviews and updates the list, if needed, with as few people as possible. Weekly sprint playbacks (described below) include anyone who has an item to work on within the sprint and maybe key leaders. Developers and product managers attend a short (15 minutes is the goal) daily stand-up meeting where they discuss any blockers to progress or issues. They schedule separate meetings if issues need to get worked out versus trying to work them out in the larger meeting which ties up the entire team.

At the end of each full sprint, the team does a dog and pony show (sprint playback) where a broader set of participants are invited to be informed and then give feedback on what was delivered. This is oftentimes a lot of fun as it is exciting to see the team progress. It creates a sense of team and allows the members to celebrate. The team also provides a retrospective perspective on what they could have done better so they can incorporate that into the next sprint.

What I am looking for on the burndown:

1. Are there any spikes in the burndown? A spike in the burndown means scope was added. Sometimes it means the work on the burndown was defined late or was never fully defined in the first place. There may be a good reason for the scope to have changed, but it is important to understand if and how often this is happening.

2. Am I ahead or behind on the overall schedule? A burndown provides a very clear view of whether or not I am ahead or behind schedule.

3. Are there any blockers? A blocker is anything that slows or stops the work. Although blockers will not be on the burndown chart, they should be listed along with the burndown. Blockers need to be resolved to avoid project delay.

As I transitioned the teams to the Agile process, one by one, some caught on immediately and others struggled. On one team, the assigned product owner told me that building an ordered list of what needs to be done was "in the weeds." He was a strategic thinker so I asked him more directly, "How can anyone execute his brilliant strategy if he could not get it on paper or communicate it to anyone else?" He had no answer for that. It became obvious to both him and me, he was not in the right role. A successful product owner is not high-level, but always in the details of defining what is in the sprint and whether or not it is ready for the team member assigned to the task.

If you are using Agile, then your team should be able to report on a critical metric called development velocity sprint. Development velocity measures the actual time to complete a task versus the estimated time to complete within a sprint. Some Agile tools require a couple of sprints before they will report velocity so beware that for new teams it may not be immediately adapted. What you are looking for is adaptation to velocity reporting up and down your organization and explanations for why velocity is changing. Sometimes a couple of developers are on vacation or a software bug took much longer to fix than expected. I typically do not really care about the reason and instead look for whether or not the team has a handle on what is going on and what the root causes of the changes are.

Takeaways:

- If a team is using Agile, they should have a burndown readily available.
- The burndown should be an integrated burndown, not siloed to only the development process.
- Have a clear product owner (quarterback) who is managing the sprint. The product owner is like the quarterback in American football, so choose well.
- Sprint playbacks are important, providing both visibility and accountability.
- Assign the right talent to manage the process.
- Development velocity does not matter, but knowing why it is changing does.

Artifacts:

Download Agile Sprint Playback Example

Download Agile Process on a Page

Discipline for Requirements and Design

You will get more on this in the product and design chapters but let me first introduce a significant problem in the software industry. I am not sure why an entire industry decided to call themselves "engineers" and then threw away just about every principle of the engineering discipline. Mechanical, civil, electrical, and chemical engineers are maniacal about both designing and defining very detailed requirements using methods that produce consistent results. Engineers in these areas are licensed and have to meet certain standards to both obtain and maintain their licensing. Given the amount of time and money that is spent on software, it is surprising that many product teams lack the rigor and process to clearly define requirements and put them on paper. People in the software industry should not call themselves engineers until they start behaving like them. Mechanical, civil, electrical, and chemical engineers should protest and demand that the designation of their discipline not be used by imposters. It is not all bad, the software in certain industries such as medical device, aviation, and automotive industries have been forced to have diligence around software requirements (as someone could die if their software fails), but they have treated user interface design as an afterthought so even these industries need improvements to their overall approach. Although I did not single-handedly invent the approach for software engineering, I describe the areas that are non-negotiable and necessary to getting products shipped quicker than anyone else in the industry. In the product and design chapters I will discuss this further and describe requirements as "well-baked," a term I created to bring home the point that requirements need to be complete.

PRODUCT

I had just sold a company to IBM about 4 months earlier and because no one knew what to do with the former CEO, and I had agreed to stay for at least two years, I sought another role and soon became the VP of Product within the company's software unit. At the time, the unit was called Watson IoT. There were a lot of products, many still in the early stage producing little to no revenue, but the software unit overall was climbing towards a billion dollars in software revenue. The company had been investing in IoT, so many of the early-stage products were the team's ideas to leverage IoT. Kudos to IBM for fostering a culture of innovation and letting the teams innovate using IoT.

In my self-introduction deck, I set one of my key goals as becoming world-class in product organization. I also explained to my new team my overall philosophy on running a product organization. Defining "world class" would cause a lot of debate amongst a room full of software executives, so it was a bit bold for me to make these statements. In a large organization, especially this one, where there had been a long history of how to manage products, I believed I had nothing to lose. I was convinced the organization had a lot of room to grow. It turns out that the organization did in fact have a lot of room to grow.

Let's start with how I define "world class." World class in my view is measured by outputs from the product teams in terms of raw output and less measurable "signals" from stakeholders of a product. These are items I use to determine if the product team has reached world class status. Stakeholders are both internal, such as sales and marketing, or external, your customers. Here are the critical signals I have utilized to determine if "world class" status has been achieved:

- Trusted advisors
- Established expertise
- Output quality
- Well-baked requirements

Note: As you progress through this and other chapters, you will notice I use the term "stakeholders" to define a set of individuals. A stakeholder is anyone who interacts with the end-to-end product process. This includes customers, technology and ecosystem partners, development, design, support, sales, technical sales, marketing, communications, executives in the company, or even investors. Now, onto defining the signals that show you are achieving world class status.

Trusted Advisor

One of the best proof points is that stakeholders see the product team as a trusted advisor, not only for the product but for advice on the best way to operate their business. If the stakeholder is a customer, then they will seek you out to learn how to streamline their business and periodically even include your product team as an advisor on an important business decision. If the stakeholder is from your sales team, then they seek you out to help with an important sales meeting or include you as a key part of their annual sales kick-off. Services will include you in decisions on how to accelerate helping customers achieve value faster and will give signals they depend on you to assist in making the best decisions for the product. Customer support will want to work with you to help streamline their efforts and solve product issues that are causing costly fixes. Stakeholders from customer success will ask for the product team to be involved in customer account planning or will include you on a call with one of their account executives.

Becoming "world class" will increase the demands on an organization. This could result in an organization being unable to achieve its core mission. To mitigate this in larger organizations, I separated my resources into two categories: Go-to-Market (GTM) and product owners. This allows product owners the space to coordinate getting fixes and features into the product.

Supporting other teams is important, but so is the company's objective. Therefore, it becomes a question of how to remain best-in-class and stay on target.

Established Expertise

The second sign, after being a trusted advisor, is that stakeholders will describe the product team as extremely helpful, responsive, or as experts in their area. This is an outcome of the product team being both accurate and responsive. When a product team is not functioning well, sales among other stakeholders are not shy about communicating their dissatisfaction with a poorly run product team. In organizations where I have taken over, there have almost always been individuals hiding out in the product organization not producing much output. This is costly for any business. While the organization can and should have some junior product managers, the reality is that the product team is making decisions that will drive the spending of millions of dollars. Therefore, both who is on the team and the decisions they are making should be taken seriously.

Output Quality

A third sign of being world class is the overall quality of the output coming from the product team. For example, if the product team creates high quality (level one) sales presentations the messaging will be clear, there will be alignment across internal teams, and customers will stick. Great b2b (business to business) software delivers results to customers. There will be customers jumping out of their seats excited about what the software is doing for their business, and happy customers will also be willing to publicly talk about it. Some other examples are high quality product pages, superior demos, and leading the market with superior messaging. In terms of the actual product, the outcome of a highly functioning product team is a visible progression of product development week by week. A well-managed product, design, and development process will run circles around competitors which I find quite fun to watch.

Well-Baked Requirements

The last sign of a world class product organization is that they produce what I call "well-baked requirements" and have a clearly communicated product roadmap. I will go into greater detail on both of these in the later sections.

So, what are the warning signs that an organization is not world class?

What I have seen is an extremely high variability in product teams inside of software companies. Some signs that your product organization may need help includes:

1. Poor revenue growth
2. Unhappy customers, which is reflected by cancellations or poor NPS scores
3. Infrequent product roadmap updates (or no product roadmap)
4. Bloated team but little to no output from the product team
5. Slow output from the software development team
6. Software developers not having clarity on what they need to build
7. Limited (or no) UX designers
8. Limited interaction between the product team and actual customers
9. Lack of coordination between GTM activities and the product team
10. High volume of support-related issues

The product organization is a critical function in any software company. Due to the complexity of managing a product, it is more difficult to recover from a poorly run product organization than it is to fix a poorly run sales organization.

If you are discouraged about your current situation at this point and are wondering how you will ever get to world class status, there is hope at the end of the tunnel. For example, within a few weeks working at a startup I was surprised to learn the company only had a few half-baked products. After approximately five years and 100 million dollars invested, the company had little to offer in terms of products.

It got worse several weeks later when a majority of the executive team quit all at once demanding to the board that the CEO step down. This included the VP of product who I knew from a previous company. It was horrible timing for me personally as my wife was pregnant and I had been working with a builder who just ripped the roof off our house to add a second story. My pregnant wife was not very excited about the prospect of me being unemployed. Then the executives who quit asked me to resign at the same time to force the existing CEO's hand. It was in the early 2000s and many companies were shedding staff, especially in Austin, TX as we were in the middle of the collapse of the .com boom. Very few tech companies were hiring, if any. My only path forward was to fix what was there and to get some real products launched to get revenue flowing into the company.

The first thing we did was to revert back to basics; streamlining the product, design, and development functions. In situations like these, there is usually some useful Internet Protcol (IP). Thankfully, that was true in this instance. The working IP consisted of routing and scheduling, Geographic Information Systems (GIS), and an appointment scheduling engine. The problem was that the whole system only ran on a PC. There were a handful of projects that were in process, but without a functioning product they did not have a high chance of being successful. There was a broad market for routing and scheduling software for service technicians, so if we could get a solution to market we would then be well-positioned for double-digit growth.

The entire process started with creating use cases and then prototyping desired solutions from companies in our target market. At the time there were no sophisticated tools to prototype screens. The work was done in Photoshop as we wanted to create what we referred to as photo-realistic screens. Over a very short period, we prototyped a scheduling module, an appointment scheduling module, and screens for a technician to view and download schedules (it was still early days for mobile applications, they would arrive later). The initial screens we created were used to have conversations with prospective customers. They were also used to validate with customers who had already engaged with us that we were building the right thing.

We rapidly iterated through prototypes as customers gave us feedback. The team also used the prototype to do some user testing. This was before screen sharing, video conferencing, and the ability to record user sessions. We instead used rooms with two-way mirrors where the team could observe how the user interacted with the software while a user researcher prompted the user to "think out loud." Nowadays, that would probably be considered creepy. Once we achieved an acceptable level of product market fit, usability and alignment with our lead customers, we began development of an entirely new product that would be the future of the company.

Once the product development was put in motion, part of the team started fixing the company's messaging, website, customer presentation and overall sales and marketing strategy. The end result: Over the next few years, with a team of less than ten people, we shipped several well-designed and fully-baked software modules that formed a suite of products to drive the company's growth. As a small team, along with some cost cutting, we were also able to make the company profitable. It was also easier to get to profitability when we no longer had the overhead of expensive software executives who had all quit at once. The company was later acquired, and the products are still in the market today and have continued to improve over time.

As I said initially, defining world class can be subjective. Each organization, its culture, and its products are unique so you have to determine what world class looks like for your company. I have merely provided some signs you can look for when working this out for you and your team. I also provided some signs of whether or not your organization is or is not operating as a world class product organization. There is unfortunately more to it than just declaring you are world class. This is where the forthcoming information on Agile, requirements, go-to-market, and design will come in handy as they cover the day-to-day on how to execute at a high level in a software company. So let's move forward and dig into the details.

Takeaways:

- The product organization is a critical part of any software company, and striving to make it world class should be a core competency.
- Define what for you is considered world class and set a plan in motion to get there.
- There is hope at the end of the tunnel.

Stakeholder Communication

Communication is essential for success in just about every endeavor. And it holds especially true in achieving that world-class ranking we discussed earlier. But in software, there are specific areas I like to focus on:

- Roadmaps
- Enhancement Request Tracking
- Value Maximization
- Release Notes

Roadmaps

I strongly believe that product roadmaps should be provided to customers quarterly at user group meetings and through online updates for and by my teams. Some companies, such as Salesforce, even go as far as publishing a more detailed list of what is in or out for a given release. Customer roadmaps should also include two years into the future as most companies are working on strategic plans in the one to three-year timeframe. Understand, your customers need to plan, and if there are gaps between their strategy and your product, your roadmap allows them to discuss alignment issues with your product team.

Enhancement Requests

I also believe it should be very clear to both internal and external stakeholders where an enhancement request can be submitted. I find it is helpful to have a section in the product for any software users to submit product ideas (or bugs). This is best practice. Do not over-burden this screen with a million questions. Make it really easy for a customer to submit a potential feature.

Value Maximization

Another form of essential communication includes information on how to get more value out of your products. This can be delivered on a help portal, via emails, video, or on customer-only webinars. I would not publish this on Youtube or any other public site as competitors will see and replicate your screens. Helpful tips are especially useful for aging software products. This approach supports that while you modernize the software, you can ease their day-to-day pain with some useful tips. This will do wonders to extend the life cycle of your software, even for products that are never going to be modernized.

Release Notes

Customers should also be sent "release notes" that typically list what is in the current release of the product. This can include both features and major bug fixes. Surprisingly, many software companies are not taking credit for all the hard work they have done to enhance their product.

A more modern approach is to provide useful tips within the software. Lightly point the user to a new feature view, or call out on the screen to a new or existing capability they have not yet used. There are now tools available that make this extremely easy to implement, but beware, they can also have security flaws. They could be attempting to capture detailed user information to send back to a server for reporting.

I would refrain from sending customers marketing-related emails as much as possible. Sometimes it is needed, if you are launching a new module for example, but these emails are more likely to result in customers unsubscribing from your list since they already own the software and you are not doing anything to add value to their day-to-day lives. Send them emails that can help them improve their day-to-day work and they will open and read them. Use clear titles that relate to things they do or could do in the software every day, versus making them look like another marketing email.

Also, in your stream of communication keep your sales team in the loop, but do not bombard them with constant communication. Especially in large organizations, requests can come from many different directions. Take the approach that sales reps should be out selling and that their time needs to be optimized. You should realize that most sales reps will not read long PowerPoint presentations or documents you send them.

Takeaways:

- A software product should have a roadmap, release notes, and a way to submit and track enhancement requests; anything less and I would not consider it to be a fully commercialized software.
- Do not pass up the opportunity to provide value to your customers (and to take credit for value that you have already delivered).
- Do not spam customers with marketing emails, they do not typically work.

Artifacts:

Download Example Software Product Roadmap

Product Requirements

I have been using a concept that I call "well-baked" requirements. I define it as providing a developer 90% of what they need to spend 90% of their time coding. I can go into any software company and ask the software developers what percentage of their time they spend directly coding versus other tasks. Most will say 50%. These developers are not using well-baked requirements and it is costing the company time and money.

Writing software requirements with clarity is a lost art. I have seen product teams write high-level product requirements that could be interpreted fifty different ways and then hand them off to the software development team.

I first learned how to write requirements while implementing software at a pharmaceutical company. If you have ever experienced this, you are forever changed. All systems in an FDA validated facility must go through a series of checkpoints to ensure the system is working as intended. For a manufacturing site implementation, we created an entire office wall covered in post-it's full of requirements and test cases. The quality assurance team at the site would go through every requirement to ensure it was unambiguous. Although I could not see myself spending my life generating endless amounts of paperwork for regulatory purposes, the process was good training for how to write clear and concise requirements.

I then further learned how to write requirements at a small startup where the development lead would take the use cases I wrote and redline them like an ambitions middle school teacher. He would take me through line-by-line what else he needed before the development team could begin coding. My use cases were already more detailed than most, so I at first did not appreciate his critiques. Add to that, he always seemed to be in a bad mood, so I often refered to him anonymously as "Grumpy Nathan." Over time, I began to appreciate Grumpy Nathan as he taught me how to effectively write requirements for developers. Eventually as I progressed skill-wise, I turned it into a game to see if I could stump him and produce such clear requirements that he could not find a single thing to redline. Grumpy Nathan rarely gave me that honor. I think he had to mark up something almost every time to ensure my ego did not explode.

That said, let's get into the details; the following are best practices for managing requirements:

- Use Clear and Precise Language
- Invoke Stakeholders
- Organize Requirements
- Be Specific
- Be Consistent

- Include Functional Requirements
- Address Non-Functional Requirements
- Consider Compliance Regulatory Requirements
- Include Interface and Integration Requirements
- Define Clear Acceptance Criteria
- Have Traceability
- Review and Revise
- Implement Approval Process
- Document and Control
- Leverage User Story Mapping and/or Use Case Maps

Use Clear and Precise Language

Not everyone has experience at a pharmaceutical plant, where it is best to use clear, concise, and

Requirement Type	Stakeholder
Use Case Requirements	Development Team, Designers, Testers, Technical Writers
System Requirements	Architects, Development Team
Compliance	Operations, Compliance Team
Scalability Requirements	Performance Testers, Architects, Development Team

unambiguous language. This standard should be used by all industries. A good source for learning how to write concise requirements is Incose.org. Their standard is used by plane manufacturers whose failure to write clear requirements can cause a plane to crash. A lot can be learned from both the pharmaceutical and systems engineering industries where clear requirements are life or death.

Download The Incose.org Guide
(*Incose Requirements*, 2023):

In addition to learning how to write with clarity, try to avoid jargon or technical terms that might be unclear to some stakeholders and use terminology that is familiar to the audience. Into one software product we embedded definitions because the industry we were launching the software for used more acronyms than a military briefing.

Once you learn to write clear requirements, work through the process of gathering and managing requirements. Do not overthink this. At the end of the day, getting something down on paper allows you to have a purposeful discussion.

Involve Stakeholders: Engage all relevant stakeholders, customers, engineers, sales reps, support personnel, domain experts, and the design team, in the requirements gathering process. Their input will ensure that the requirements capture the diverse needs and concerns of different parties. Show them prototyped screens, visit users in the environment where they use the software, involve designers on customer calls or have them attend user conferences. At one conference, we set up a solution center where any customer could come and discuss what they would like the software to do. We also did back- to-back user testing throughout the conference. In a startup, you do not have that many resources to involve, so it may be the founder writing the initial requirements who then goes out and seeks input from peers, customers, investors.

Organize Requirements:

Group requirements logically in your documentation, separating them into categories, such as use case (user), system, compliance (such as ISO or regulatory) and scalability requirements. This makes it easier for the stakeholders who will consume these requirements to locate and understand specific aspects of the solution.

Be Specific

Avoid vague requirements. Specify exact details of what the system should or should not do. Include specific use cases, workflow charts, and scenarios to illustrate how the system will be used. If screens are involved, produce high-fidelity designs for each screen. Here is an example:

Vague requirement Example:

A user will have the ability to log into the solution using a valid username.

Complete requirement(s):

A user will have the ability to log into the system using a valid email address as their username.

An email address is a unique identifier for an email inbox to which messages are delivered.

An email shall consist of two parts: the user and the domain name.

Here is an example of a valid email address: user@domain.com.

The user comes before the @ symbol and identifies the recipient of the email.

The domain name comes after the @ symbol and identifies the email provider or organization hosting the email account.

The user can contain letters, digits, and special characters such as !#$%&'*±/=?^_`{|}~.

The user cannot begin or end with a period (.), nor can it contain two consecutive periods.

The domain name can contain letters, digits, hyphens (-), and periods (.)

A domain name cannot begin or end with a hyphen, nor can it contain two consecutive periods.

Although this is rare (incomplete requirements tend to be the norm), I have run into teams who turn product managers into full-time feature writers, breaking down everything into excessive detail when it is not necessary. For example, one development team required the product team to create a ticket for the outline color of an input field. The design team provided them with stylesheets that clearly specified this, therefore, creating a ticket specifically for this was dumb as the developers were already provided with very specific requirements for this. Well-baked means "exactly" what a developer needs, nothing "less" nor nothing "more" than what they need.

Use a Consistent Format

Adopt a consistent format for presenting requirements. This might include a unique identifier for each requirement, a clear description, and any relevant acceptance criteria. I tend to associate my user requirements with a use case.

Example: Use Case 100 - Login to Software

Requirements:

100.1 A user will have the ability to log into the system using a valid email address as their username.

100.2 An email address is a unique identifier for an email box to which messages are delivered.

{the rest of the requirements were not copied in - see above}

Use Case Map Example

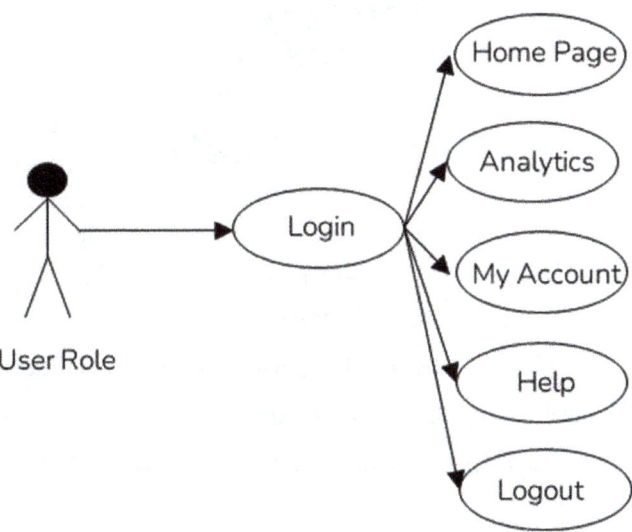

Artifacts:

Download Example Use Case Requirements

Download Example Use Case Map

I prefer use cases. Others prefer user story mapping. I have tried user story mapping but ran into the issue that user stories are really good for users, not software developers. If you provide user stories, you have to provide additional details Grumpy Nathan will need somewhere else.

Include Functional Requirements

Functional requirements define what the system should do. Describe the expected behaviors, features, and interactions the system must support. For example, specify how the system should handle data input, process data, and generate reports.

Address Non-Functional Requirements

Non-functional requirements cover aspects like performance, security, usability, reliability, and scalability. Clearly state the minimum performance benchmarks, security protocols, and other quality attributes that the system must adhere to. I tend to include all of the non-functional requirements into a single requirements document that I title "System Requirements." You may include non-functional requirements in other requirements documents, such as the user requirements, but be sure to track them and include them in the System Requirements. A common issue is that these requirements do not get prioritized but the software development team knows this work is important so they carve out developers to do this work. Sometimes they do not balance this work against other feature work and it makes feature development look slow, creating tension between the product and development team. Transparency is a better approach. Or even worse, this important work never gets done and issues occur in production.

Download Example System Requirements

Consider Compliance and Regulatory Requirement

You must ensure that your system requirements align with relevant regulations and guidelines, such as General Data Protection Regulation (GDPR), International Organization for Standardization (ISO) standards, and accessibility requirements among others. Address how the system will ensure compliance and data integrity.

Include Interface and Integration Requirements

Specify how the system will integrate with other systems. Define data exchange formats, communication protocols, and any interoperability requirements in a system requirements document. Define requirements in the user interface. For example, should the screens be responsive? Will they be viewed on a mobile phone? Which phones?

Define Clear Acceptance Criteria

Each requirement should have clear acceptance criteria that define when the requirement is considered satisfied. This helps in verifying the system during development and testing. In software user requirements based on use cases, the postcondition tends to be the acceptance criteria.

Traceability

If needed, establish traceability or links between requirements to demonstrate how each requirement supports high-level business or user needs. This ensures that nothing is overlooked and helps in impact analysis when changes are made.

Review and Revise

Regularly review and revise the requirements with stakeholders. This helps to ensure that the requirements remain accurate and up-to-date as the project progresses. The teams I manage do this via requirements, solutions, and design playbacks.

Have An Approval Process

If possible, ensure that the final set of requirements is reviewed before they are given to teams to design or develop. Keep it light and easy where a PM (Product Manager) or product owner can approve a sprint (unless you are working in a regulated environment). I tend to operate with small teams who are both qualified and empowered to make decisions, avoiding a bottle-necked decision making and approval process. If the requirements are compliance related, define who can verify compliance with industry standards and regulations.

Document Change Control

Establish a change control process to manage any updates or modifications to the requirements. This is where software tools such as Jira or Aha! come in handy. If in a highly regulated environment, a solution such as IBM Engineering Requirements (known as DOORS) helps. Changes should be carefully documented, reviewed, and approved by relevant stakeholders if the requirements have been materially changed.

User story mapping

I prefer use cases and Unified Modeling Language (UML), but user story mapping takes its place. User story mapping is great when defining how a solution will interact with users (hence why it is called "user" story mapping). User story mapping does not produce well-baked or complete requirements as it excludes information a developer would need to develop the solution.

Takeaways

- Writing well-baked requirements is the difference between developers spending 50% vs 90%+ of their time coding.
- Learn how to write clear, concise and complete requirements.
- Find a grumpy Nathan. Ok, they don't have to be grumpy, but find a developer who can teach you what a developer needs.
- Have a process for managing requirements, including change control.
- Don't overdo it and create mountains of unnecessary "electronic" paperwork in the form of tickets.

Product Roadmaps

This may sound ridiculous but my first rule for product roadmaps (summary of the vision and direction of your product over time) is to "have one roadmap at all times." Yes, this actually has to be said. Anyone who has worked in the software industry will understand why I am saying this. After taking over a large product portfolio I became a dictator concerning roadmaps. I immediately required all of my product teams to provide me with product roadmaps and then update them at least once a quarter. I even assigned a person to work across all the teams to make sure this happened.

Many product teams are reluctant to put product plans on paper as things change, especially in today's world. This unfortunately does not provide an excuse for not communicating with all of the stakeholders of your product as to what your plan for the product is. Lack of communication and transparency leads to a lack of trust and commitment. If you want a company that does not trust its product team and customers who are not committed to your product, then do not publish a product roadmap.

After asking for their product roadmap, many of the teams did not come back to me until months after my initial request. Some of them came back with something so high-level I wound up telling them they better get more specific very soon or I would move their R&D resources to teams who had a clear plan for their product. Not only did I require regular publishing and updates to product roadmaps, but I also required that they include at least two years in the future. Why two years? Many of my customers did their strategic planning two years out and providing a two-year view of my product allowed them to plan better. The same applied to my business partners, some of whom were making investments in bolt-on solutions or investing in building out consulting practices based on my product direction. A two-year roadmap allowed them to plan better and avoid channel conflicts.

Jimmy Buffet, the singer, said "Indecision may or may not be my problem."

If you are a product company, you have to pick a lane. It does not mean that you cannot turn the corner or get into another lane later. Indecision goes both ways. You can change lanes every other day and create one set of problems or you can never get on the highway and therefore never pick a lane in the first place. The key is to have a lane and have everyone inside and outside of your company aligned with you on the road. Indecision and lack of clarity on the product direction creates confusion that then leads to customers abandoning your solution and employees leaving your company.

Decide how much time is needed to ensure that the company and team are on the right path. Then decide whether or not the path is leading to the desired outcome. Also, provide clarity to your team on how they will know if they are on the right path or not.

A famous example of not understanding the product path one is on is the Blackberry story. The team and leadership failed over and over again to understand that the iPhone, along with the platform it provided for software developers to produce new applications and generate revenue, was going to change the cell phone market forever. Before the iPhone, it seemed that everyone had a Blackberry. I actually switched because the design for the keyboard on the Blackberry was so good. In fact, I spent too much time responding to emails during non-working hours because of that keyboard. They called Blackberry phones "crackberries" and I was addicted.

However, I eventually switched to an iPhone because it was harder/slower to type emails using their keyboard. Yep, after switching to an iPhone I spent less time on my phone while at home. The product team at RIM thought that no one would stitch to the iPhone interface because it was more cumbersome to use. RIM CEO's famous last words of "We'll be fine" (Olson, 2015) have gone down in history as one of the worst examples of not knowing you are on the wrong path.

***To think through general areas of investment I use a tool called an investment matrix. It compares the amount of value (or savings) I am delivering to my customer as compared to the amount of revenue it will generate for my company over the next five years. This is based on the belief that the more value I deliver to my customers, the more revenue I will generate for my company. Customers pay for value. The items in the upper right-hand corner are typically the best areas to invest in. It does not always mean that something in the lower left does not make the list. Some items are considered bread and butter items so they are needed, regardless of the value they produce for either me or my customers. But you want to minimize these investments as much as possible.

PRODUCT | 109

The size of the investment is specified by the size of the bubble on the chart. In my example, a medium-sized bubble is a five million dollar investment over the same five-year period as the revenue. I am then looking for three to four times the total investment in revenue over the next five years. A five million dollar investment should produce $15-20 million in revenue for an established product. Not all investments will produce this type of yield but this should be the target.

In the end, it was not enough just to require product teams in this organization to have a two-year roadmap. I required each team to publish its own roadmap. We did this regularly by distributing product roadmaps to sales, support, and customer success teams. For customers, we presented product roadmaps at user conferences and provided them when customers requested them.

Ideally there is a schedule, such as quarterly, in which product roadmaps get published. Salesforce is a best-in-class example in that they announce publicly every quarter what made it into the next quarter's product release and more importantly, what didn't make it. They make an event of this, poking most of the other software companies in the eye who are doing a poor job of communicating and being transparent with their customers.

Once I established product roadmaps, I dug into how teams were capturing features from customers. Many software products make this way too difficult. I believe a customer should be able to request a feature from within the product itself, ideally in the context in which they are using the software. We designed a simple screen to log a feature from within our software and gave it to all of my product teams. Some basic questions are:

- How many software products do this? Very few. We also included guidance on where to place this capability to ensure every user of the software would discover their ability to give us feedback.
- How long did it take my product teams to get back to our customers when a feature was requested?
- When they did follow up with our customers, were they clear?
- Did they provide a yes, no, or "maybe, but I need more info" answer?

I was embarrassed to learn that most customers never received a response and when they did it was not even remotely a clear yes, no, or maybe. Requests were piling up in our ticketing system. Some were two years old and were never reviewed. In a well-run product team feature requests come in and get triaged on a cadence. If product teams are not making decisions or feature requests from customers what exactly are we doing? I am not sure I ever figured that out, but I can tell you they became responsive very quickly, and in some cases they had to pour through requests from customers from the past two years and make yes or no decisions on them immediately. If they chose "maybe," they had to convert the maybe to a yes or no in 90 days. I called the backlog of not responding to customers, and past due homework.

Takeaways:

- Publish roadmaps regularly, no less than once a quarter.
- Indecision is problematic, therefore, avoid it (I am kidding, "be decisive!")
- Make it easy to capture feature requests from customers, preferably directly from within your product.
- The product team should have agreed to Service Level Agreements (SLA) for how quickly they respond to customer feature requests.
- Leverage an investment matrix to think through major areas of investment.
- Customer feature requests should get an answer for every request: yes, no, or yes but it is outside of our x-year roadmap answer for every request (no maybe's).
- Roadmaps should match a customer's planning cycle, therefore, if customers plan out investments for 2-3 years, then your product roadmap should match this timeline.

Example Artifacts:

Download Product Roadmap Template

Download Investment Matrix Template

Product Naming

Often, product naming is heavily tied to company naming. If your company has a strong brand already, then you do not need to establish yet another brand. In this circumstance, it is best to just name product modules in a way that describes exactly what they do. I have named a lot of products and this is always a stressful exercise for the organization. Everybody in the company has an opinion. Here are the guidelines I have established:

- If your company already has a strong brand, do not waste time or money creating a new one with your product naming (for example, Adobe has a strong brand so the products leverage the brand name).

- If your company is new and does not have a brand, simplify as much as possible and follow similar rules for product naming, like the one-word rule. You most likely will not be able to name the company in a descriptive way as most domain names are already owned by someone else and purchasing one could be expensive. Company naming is complex. Therefore, you then have to spend time establishing the brand. Examples: Apple, Chase. Who wants to Chase their bank or would associate a computer with food such as an Apple? Over time they worked. Salesforce was brilliant in terms of simplicity as it named both the company and the product.

- Call the product exactly what it is and does. Your marketing and SEO team will thank you for that. For example, IBM Maximo is a suite of products and we named one of the modules Mobile and another Predict. Maximo manages assets and is a solution for maintenance technicians, so everyone knows who the mobile was for (technicians) and that Predict is doing predictive failures for assets. Note that we already had strong brands in IBM and Maximo, which allowed us to focus on describing what the product did.

- Try to name your product with one word that is short, simple, and easy to remember. For example, SAP's next-generation ERP is called S4 or sometimes S4/Hana as they try to promote their database.

- If you cannot name your product with one word, then do so with two words, but focus on the easy-to-remember concept. Try to have the second word further explain the product. Examples are the Adobe Creative Suite, and the Microsoft Office Suite.

- Consider it extreme to name a product with three words. Many people, including me, will not be able to remember the name of it. I have made exceptions for products that can be abbreviated. For example, at IBM we named a product Environmental Intelligence Suite but everyone calls it EIS which is still one simple "word."

- Pick a product name
- Do a trademark search, if there is an actual conflict, go to step 1
- Perform SEO analysis, if an issue, go to step 1.
- Put the name out there and deal with lots of input (good luck!)
- Rest - well done. Quit second guessing yourself.

With any company or product naming you will have to make sure you are not in violation of any trademarks. Avoid costly errors and do a trademark search. You can go to https://www.uspto.gov/trademarks and search quickly, but I recommend leveraging a trademark attorney. Your product name may be taken, but a brand qualifier can remove a trademark conflict. A trademark attorney can advise you if there is a conflict. Getting a letter asking you to quit using someone else's trademark is not fun. Luckily, I have not yet had to deal with that for a product I have named, but I have had to deal with it for products named prior to my joining a company.

Additionally, I am always surprised when companies do not bother to do a simple keyword search to see how competitive their product name will be in major search engines such as Google, Bing, Quora, or DuckDuckGo. Even worse, sometimes, unexpected results appear in search results. You do not want to compete with the latest porn site or pop star in your SEO competition. Naming your product in a way that describes what it does will drastically help with SEO. If you can afford it, it is worth filing trademarks for major geographies where you plan to do business.

Now, it is rare to have an issue, but you should also consider what your product name means when it is translated into other languages. When it is an issue, it is REALLY an issue. I would typically check the top 9 languages spoken globally. If your company only plans to do business in the US, then don't bother, but most software companies want to scale globally at some point. Siri, Apple's assistant, when translated into Georgian is something vulgar. Yikes!

Artifacts:

Download Trademark Search

Competitors

My view of competitors is that my team should have "their ears to the ground." This reference comes from watching old western movies where Native Americans would put their ear to the ground and hear someone, an enemy usually, coming from miles away. They noticed everything. A broken branch, footprints, animal tracks, or breadcrumbs the enemy dropped along the way. Like the Native Americans, I do this because I do not want to be ambushed. There are "listening" tools out there that can help. One common and easy way to listen to the ground is to use Google alerts at alerts.google.com. It will send to your inbox any mention of a particular keyword.

Keeping your ear to the ground is essential but don't overreact. It becomes comical to see how a sales rep, board member, or executive in my company reacts to what competitors are doing. This typically creates an avalanche of activity that sends my team in what is often the wrong direction. Having seen these misdirects enough times, I decided we should send our competitors on goose chases, and keep my employees on task. Who is the goose in this instance? Just because a competitor is doing something it does not mean you should be doing the exact same thing (see the discussion on market segmentation in the Marketing chapter). In reality, the market is typically big enough for more than one company.

Based on your revenue goals, how many customers do you need to add? Why go head-to-head with the competition 100% of the time, when hitting your revenue targets may not necessitate you going head-to-head with a competitor at all. There will always be competition, but don't waste precious time in a battle if it's not warranted. Some may have hundreds of millions of dollars (often my competition) while you are minimally funded. With what I am going to tell you next, it does not necessarily matter that your competitor is better funded. Go out and execute better than them.

You can beat the competition with focused execution. Early in my career I was helping to launch and grow the SAP practice with Ernst & Young. This was before anyone knew the firm even needed an SAP practice. To help our win rate, I ran a Center of Excellence that managed all of the template deliverables used by projects. One of the items I collected was all of our customer proposals.

One day, while looking for a "winning" proposal, I noticed that the thicker the proposal the higher the probability that we lost the bid. Huh? Some of our largest projects were the thinnest proposals. The fatter the proposal and the more resources we spent, the higher the probability that we lost the deal. I knew that because I also ultimately controlled all the resources in that part of the practice, I knew who was assigned to which project, including sales efforts.

I started to compare our sales efforts to romance dating, especially when someone was asking me for an inordinate number of resources for a sales effort. Everything in dating is good in the beginning. The person you take on the first date is amazing, otherwise you would not be going out on a date. As time goes on you learn their bad habits and annoyances. The more time spent, the more reasons you learn not to date that person. Certainly, there is true love which then allows you to look past someone's faults but this is not the same with a customer. They are looking for a reason to not hire you. The sooner you know this, the smarter you become.

Therefore, narrow your focus and give the customer fewer reasons to rule your product out. As a reminder, this is only one area where better execution can help you win. Others areas include hiring and retaining better talent, creating and delivering better messaging, creating and supporting a better user experience, and delivering a better technology architecture.

In addition to proposals, one of the GTMt deliverables is called a competitive battlecard. This is a short summary or background about a competitor and how to win against them. This helps bolster the confidence of sales representatives. Although your execution may be better, sales people can still be spooked by competitors. I would recommend that you also include a reminder to never slander. As a rule of thumb I tell my sales people to never say anything bad about a competitor in front of a customer. Bad mouthing the competition never works because customers do not like negativity, even if the competitor is nowhere near as good as you or your company.

If a customer brings up a competitor I will give them a positive pat-on-the-back but with a slant in my favor. For example, if the chemical industry customer I am talking with mentions a competitor I will reply that the competition "is really good in the retail sector." Which in this instance is a true statement, the competition is really good in the retail industry. Notice, I did not say anything bad about my competitor, but in the head of my customer they are now wondering what their experience is in the chemical industry and with a little bit of research, the customer will quickly learn they have no experience in this area.

Takeaways:

- Keep your ear to the ground; know what your competitors are doing.
- Do not overreact to competitors' moves (actually, send THEM on a goose chase).
- Win using focused execution and the processes outlined in this entire book.
- Know the antitrust laws in the countries you operate.

Artifacts

Download Competitor Battlecard Example

THE GO-TO-MARKET TEAM

There are aspects of managing software that I have often delegate to a special team focused on the Go-to-Market (GTM) aspects of a product. This brings together the interactions with sales, marketing, product, support, and the partner teams into a cohesive approach. They operate similarly to the product delivery team in that they have an integrated Agile burn down and deliver work in sprints. I will describe this in this section, including GTM related items such as the typical GTM deliverables for a software product, market sizing, and one of the most complex aspects of GTM - driving clarity on the overall operating model for the company and products. I will first cover the go-to-market deliverables every team should be focussed on. If you are a seasoned software professional, this section can be used as a reference guide, although I am experienced and refer to my own materials when working through the GTM and operating models for new products because GTM is complex!

Download Example GTM Deliverables

Many software teams get stuck determining what to work on when. The difference between an experienced team and a rookie team is 1) the order in which they work on things and 2) the quality of the deliverables coming out of the GTM sprints. I provide free and paid examples online at https://thebookonsoftware.com to help even a rookie team produce better quality GTM deliverables. You do not need to deliver all of the GTM deliverables at once. It is easy to get distracted by someone (usually an executive) trying to insert a lower priority GTM deliverable onto the schedule sooner than you really need it. Most software teams build out the majority of these GTM deliverables. Prioritizing them and delivering them in a sequence makes the entire delivery go faster. Otherwise, your GTM team will be running around with their hair on fire, not getting much done because everything is partially complete. Now, some help on the order. I break the deliverables down into three categories:

Category 1 - Needed prior to product launch (or shortly thereafter)

Category 2 - Needed in the first 12 months

Category 3 - Delivered as time allows

Category 1

Level 1 presentation - the customer facing presentation used for the first meeting with a customer (Level 1 = meeting 1; Level 2 = meeting 2, Level 3 = meeting 3)

Messaging guide - summarizes the product and company messaging into a 30-second elevator pitch, a 2 minute summary, a 5 minute summary and a 10 minute summary of the messaging.

Product demo - the demo should be shipped at the same time as the product, otherwise, there is no point in shipping the product given you cannot sell it without a demo (besides to say that you have shipped it). Ideally a demo is a live system where the sales team or a customer can experience the software firsthand, but it could also be a clickable prototype, a product walkthrough video, or an online interactive demo.

Product brochure - Also, sometimes referred to as a product data sheet. Customers want something they can use to explain the product to other people in their company. In addition to your website, a product 1-pager (front and back) is useful for this purpose. It also makes you look like a real software company (because you are!)

Product demo script - Even if you have been heavily involved in the product and are doing the demos, I would encourage you to script out your demos. Have a larger team you need to enable? Then definitely have a demo script to help scale your best demo.

Buyer personas - Profiles of who is going to purchase the software. This is needed early to develop the sales pipeline and run targeted marketing campaigns.

Website -This includes more than just a website, it includes the lead generation and conversion process on the website.

Value Calculator - Needed even on early deals is a value calculator that helps sales and a customer work through the value of your product (to justify the purchase). If you are product-led, you have to do this in under 1-2 minutes and on your website (some argue even quicker).

2-minute video - To help explain the product and the value it creates, a 2-minute marketing video can help, especially for product-led offerings.

Lead generation strategy - A documented approach to finding leads, including a target account list on who are the potential customers of the solution.

Pricing calculator - If your pricing is not online, this helps gain alignment across teams (including finance) on the pricing for the product. The pricing calculator is what sales reps or a pricing team uses to generate quotes.

Proposal template - Be ready to produce a proposal to your early customers. Having a proposal template ready will cut days/weeks/months off the quoting cycle.

Contract template - Likewise, be ready to go with a software license agreement for your software.

Sales training - Not intentionally left last (although some sales reps will not believe me) is sales training.

Marketing strategy - Have a well-thought-out marketing strategy for the first 12- months of your product launch that details Adword and Display Ad campaigns, lead generation, events, content marketing, LinkedIn and social media campaigns, email marketing, webinars, and influencer campaigns.

Category 2

These deliverables can be delivered incrementally over the first 12 months of the product launch.

Case studies - Documented proof shows how customers are achieving value from your product.

1-page conversation guide - Assists sales reps with a 1-pager to help them sell the product. This is especially helpful when they are first learning the product or have more than one product to sell.

Technical overview - At some point in the sales process, IT may get involved, so a technical overview is needed to proactively address and answer any questions they may have.

Business case template - As part of a value study, the business case template simplifies the process of creating a business case for the customer.

References - This is a summary of written references to optimize the reference checking time. This can also be a summary of customers who are willing to be a reference for your product.

Webinar - Webinars are online events that oftentimes produce some of the best leads for certain types of software.

Competitor analysis - Helping your organization better understand and compete with competitors always pays dividends. Avoid bad-mouthing competitors in front of customers as negative selling does not work.

Qualification guide - These are a set of questions and criteria for ensuring that a customer is a good fit for your software. They are leveraged to avoid wasting both your time and the customers.

Product training - Developing training materials can be expensive so invest wisely here. Ideally design your products better so that less product training is required.

Recorded demo - This is used to train new sales engineers to demo your product. Sometimes a recorded demo is used online for potential customers.

Implementation methodology - The implementation methodology is the playbook for how to implement the software. It is usually coupled with a detailed Implementation Guide.

SOW template - statement of work template (SOW) used to provide a services estimate for projects if services are sold along with the software.

Objection responses - During the sales cycle, sales reps get objections from customers that prevent them from buying the software. Accumulate these over time and help provide better answers to these objections to increase your chances of closing a deal.

Customer testimonials - These are shorter references that are quotes or short videos that are put on your website to provide proof points of your software.

Social strategy (if applicable) - Most likely to be LinkedIn, Facebook, and Instagram a social strategy provides an online presence.

Blog post - As part of your overall content strategy, blog posts provide useful information to customers about topics that prove you are relevant as a software provider.

FAQ - Frequently asked questions are posted on the website and can both reduce support volumes and provide assistance to sales efforts. THey can also boost SEO (search engine optimization).

Category 3

These deliverables are typically built after 12+ months of being in the market. There is no reason not to deliver them sooner if you have a high performing product GTM team.

Quick reference guide - Cheat sheets to help users use the software. Not applicable to all types of software, but worthwhile when it is.

Sales process infographic - A 1-pager for sales on the overall sales process for your product. Helpful if sales representatives are selling more than one product.

Web-based ROI tool - Used as a lead engine, an online sales tool to help customers calculate value using your software.

NPS tracking - Net promoter score (or other) tracking to obtain feedback from customers. Ideally, this is implemented sooner than category three but there is also the reality that the product is new and changing early in its launch cycle so it needs to settle down a bit before NPS scoring will reflect the customer sentiment. Early on when there are less customers everyone tends to know the sentiment of these early customers.

Success tracking criteria - Metrics to track success across both an internal and external set of measures.

Benchmarking studies - Cross-industry studies used to show customers that using your product results in value or that industry segments need a product such as yours.

Implementation guide - A more detailed guide to implement the solution. This is usually created after more experience is gained implementing the software over a larger set of customers.

QBR - Quarterly business review guidelines help your customer success team meet with customers quarterly and ensure ongoing success.

Hand over process -

Analyst reports - I put this in category 3 because I am bitter towards all the analysts who did not rate me well early in my product launch cycle. Kidding aside (sort of), these are downloadable analyst reports that help generate leads from either your website or the analysts.

RFP responses - A canned set of copy and paste responses to request for proposal (RFP) questions. More likely to be needed on large and expensive software or if selling to the government.

Takeaway:

- Have a dedicated GTM team and process.
- Manage the team the same as the product delivery team, using an integrated Agile burn down including sales, sales enablement, marketing, and the product team.
- Order matters, think through the order that makes sense for your product.
- Leverage high quality examples, there is no need to reinvent the wheel.

Artifacts

Download Example GTM Deliverables GTM Deliverable Listing

Download Example GTM Deliverables GTM Burn Down

Market Sizing

Having been in the startup world for over 20 years, I have seen more market sizing than I would like. Determining the number of buyers available to your product or service can be tedious. Early in my career I was impressed by the large numbers and amount of detail in the market analysis I received. Not anymore. Today, most analysis reports contain market potential, which is what the market would be if all or a percentage of the market purchased one of my products. This is unrealistic, as it does not answer important questions.

For example, how do I know if customers are even ready to purchase my product? Do they even know they need it? Do I have to convince them of a new way to operate their business? Do not get me wrong, I do look at market potential, but I am more concerned with the "current" market that is ready for my product and how much revenue the market has actually generated in the past 12 months. I am more likely to consider the sum of my, and all my competitors revenue to be the market sizing, than I am the overall market to be my market potential.

I have watched too many of my fellow entrepreneurs launch a company only to learn that they are way ahead of the market. A co-worker launched an in-vehicle IoT tracking solution 15 years before another company did the exact same thing and had a $200M+ exit from the market. Because he was too early to market, my co-worker's company went bankrupt. What was the difference in products? The GPS tracking chips improved and did not suck the battery of a vehicle dry in 9 months. The chips also became less expensive and more accurate. Plus, the data plans became much less expensive during this 15-year timeframe. They reduced in price from approximately $100/month to $10/month. More sophisticated data compression algorithms were introduced so more data could be sent for even less money because it was compressed. Interestingly enough, GPS tracking also became more commonplace. Early on, workers would get very upset knowing they were being tracked. One of his customers' employees even poured coffee on his GPS tracker to keep it from locating him. As GPS tracking became commonplace in vehicles and even on phones, employees being tracked in a company vehicle was no longer scary and offensive. It is always interesting to see how people allow things to become commonplace when previously, they were vehemently opposed to it (i.e. being tracked via your phone).

This "too early" pattern is not unique to startups. Big Blue spent an untold amount of money chasing after areas such as blockchain and IoT. Both good ideas that eventually produced revenue, but they were way ahead of the market. A very expensive mistake.

Now that I have convinced you to not overstate your market sizing and to pay attention to market timing, I have to admit that market sizing is important to investors. It is also not a bad idea to ensure that you are investing in an area that has an adequate market size to reach your stated revenue goals. Let's break down a typical market sizing. The first thing you need to know is the total addressable market (TAM). This is the total revenue that your software product could obtain if every single company purchases your software. This is typically in the billions of dollars for most software products. Given it is not realistic for every company to purchase your software, the next step is to break down the TAM into the serviceable addressable market (SAM). This is dividing the TAM into categories of companies and the % of companies that are "likely" to purchase your software or that are "serviceable." TAM considers that companies in this market only replace their solution once over seven years, and only a certain percentage of those customers are going to look for, or be willing to purchase new software at any given time. A typical range is 15-35% of the TAM is serviceable. The next calculation defines what is obtainable. This is defined as the service obtainable market (SOM).

Operating Models

Operating models are complex and discussing them, oftentimes, results in massive confusion because going to market, billing, metering, licensing, hosting, and pricing get all twisted together. I was losing my mind trying to sort out how to deal with ensuing confusion after a late-night date with PowerPoint. I wound up creating the below cheat sheet that broke everything into lanes. My goal was to have a coherent and productive discussion across teams. Even the terminology being used was not consistent.

Operating Model Cheat Sheet

Legend: Current State | Future | Out of Scope

Go to Market Model	Usage Metering Model	Digital Metering Model	Billing Model	Licensing Model	Provisioning Model	Deployment Model	Pricing Model
Marketing Led	Install	User Experience	In Arrears	Perpetual	Hybrid	Hosted	VPC
Sales Led	OEM	User Feedback	Pre-Billed	SaaS	Self Provision	Managed Service	User
Product Led	Concurrent User	Usage	Overage Billing	CTL (Software)	SaaS	SaaS	Install
	VPC	Manage (Gainsight)	In App Purchase		In App Provisioning	Hybrid	Disk Space
	Concurrent User	Nurture (Braze)	OEM Billing		Marketplace	On Premise	Consumption
	Disk Space						

THE GO-TO-MARKET TEAM

The incremental challenge is that all these areas are interrelated. By added color coding any software product could be applied to mark the operating area as current state, out of scope, or future. This list is not comprehensive, and I am sure it is biased based on the software products I have worked on, but it is a start. You can download this as a template and update it yourself here. Let's break down each of these areas to better explain what each one is, starting with the "go-to-market model", oftentimes abbreviated as GTM.

Download Example Operating Model

Go-to-Market Model (GTM)

There are three main Go-to-Market (GTM) models for software: product-led, marketing-led, and sales-led. There is actually a fourth, embedded software, but I am not addressing that here. Using the chart below, you can see how different product-led is from marketing or sales-led. Many products you purchase directly are product-led and you may not even know it. For example, if you licensed Netflix, did you speak to a sales representative? Did you hear about it from someone else or did you see some marketing somewhere that made you aware of their service? Did Blockbuster close and leave you wondering where to get your movies? Did anyone tell you where to go?

	Product Led	**Marketing Led**	**Sales Led**
How are customers acquired?	• Word of mouth • Social shares • Network effect (invite) • Forum discussions • SEO • Website • Adwords	• Traditional Ads • Digital advertising • Analyst reports • Remarketing • Industry conferences • Online content • Press releases • Partners	• Phone calls • Demos • Customer visits • Dinners • Company events (golf) • Partner events • Conferences
How are customers retained?	• User progression • Certifications • Push notifications • Emails • Communities • Chat-bot support • Product support • Personalization • Onboarding • Incentives	• Email nurturing • User groups • Partners • In-app nurture (less common)	• Relationship management • Customer success teams (QBR) • Product Support • Renewals via billing • Renewal via sales • CEO/executive visit • User groups
How does monetization occur?	• Trials • Freemium • Onboarding process • In application pokes • Expiration emails	• Direct sales • Partner sales	• Traditional selling • Deal negotiation • Discounting

Marketing-led and sales-led GTMs are more traditional methods for selling enterprise software. The argument is that customers need interaction with a person because the sale is much too complicated for a customer to purchase these types of software products online. In many cases, those making this argument are correct. I have seen software companies take a software product that is traditionally sold sales-led, put it online with a self-sign-up process, and then watch it bomb. This is often an attempt to be like other companies who have fewer sales reps and more revenue.

One can be envious of others, but one cannot fake it. If the software was not designed to be purchased online, or if the user journey is complex, then product-led will not work. In a software solution with hundreds if not thousands of screens, the chance of a user logging in and figuring out how to use the software is not likely. Companies like Intuit were built from the ground up designed to be product-led software offerings and have the design, team, and infrastructure to make this model work.

Usage Metering Model

The usage metering model is how usage of the software is measured. This data is typically used by the operations team to help plan and scale the infrastructure on which the software runs. Usage data is most often driven by what is needed for pricing and licensing, but not always so. The software team may want to meter the solution and track one of these metrics to properly size the environments on which the software runs. The modern method of usage metering is to automate it, make it available to administrators of the software, and to utilize a "call home" feature where usage metering is reported back to a centralized server.

The argument against this is that some customers do not allow their data to be saved on an external server they do not control, especially for software that is installed on-premise. Usage metering is easy to do in a SaaS environment. I have run into situations where "air gap" support is needed. This is when you have to install the software without any access outside of the installation hardware and no usage metering is allowed. For example, a military installation may not want your software to transmit anything from their servers to anywhere.

A separate but recent example of this is the voting machines in the US. The public was surprised to find out that user metering data was being transmitted to a foreign country, in this instance, one of their adversaries. An easy way to handle this is to enable usage metering to be turned on or off. Another option is to have opt-in and opt-out support. With country laws changing this may eventually, or in some countries already, be a requirement. The list below is also not comprehensive, but it defines how some companies use their software and some of the methods used for usage metering in software:

Install	This keeps track of whether the software is installed or not. The licensing may allow multiple copies of the software to be installed e.g. for production, testing, and development.
OEM - Original Equipment Manufacturer	In this instance, a partner is selling the software and possibly white-labeling it, which means they are selling it as their software. The partner may keep track of where the software is installed.
Concurrent User	A concurrent user is logged into the system at the same time as another user. For example, 1000 users may have access to software but only 250 can log in at the same time. This works well for software that is not used all day long, but is more confusing to explain to customers.
VPC - Virtual Processing Core	This type of usage metering keeps track of the number of virtual processors on the hardware in which the software is running. You will see this type of licensing for database software, as it allows them to charge more for larger installations of their solution.
Disk Space	The metering is based on the amount of disk space being used. Google drive or a photo sharing site utilizes this approach as their costs increase when the supplier must acquire more storage space.

Digital Metering Model

Digital metering is different when used by a company's digital, growth, product design and marketing teams. Many software products lack digital metering, or it is a hodgepodge of tools bailed together. The data that digital metering can provide is valuable. Some common types of digital metering data gathered include:

User experience	This type of metering includes helpful interactions with users, prompting them to try a new feature. The goal is to make the user experience better. The first time a customer logs into the software helpful tips are provided to show the customer how to use the software. A more sophisticated model displays a started workflow, including embedded videos on how to use the software.
User feedback	User feedback can happen inside the software or via follow up emails. Direct, in-application feedback tends to be the best, but be careful not to borrow too much time from your users as they may write angry responses. The best known user feedback tool is the Net Promoter Score (NPS) but companies also use Voice of Customer Surveys and Customer Effort Scoring.
Usage	Usage keeps track of which screens, buttons, and controls are utilized and how long users spend on screens. There is always a balance between how much data to collect and the impact it will have on the performance of the software. Be aware that collecting private information may violate your license agreement and privacy laws. In some instances, it creates a security issue if a password or other sensitive information is captured.
Manage	These tools are used by the customer success, support, and product teams to manage their interactions with the customer. This can be as simple as a ticketing system or a screen for customers to submit feature requests. It can be sophisticated to include progress updates, upcoming meetings, user events, webinars or information that helps these teams manage the customer better and to help the customer be more successful using your software.
Nurture	Nurture a customer that is already using the software. Notice, I do not say license, as they may be in the freemium phase or a trial phase. The goal is to move the customer along the buying journey to purchase more of your software.

Billing Model

Now you are starting to understand what makes product management so complicated and sometimes confusing. Let's sort out another area that is often misunderstood: billing. Billing is different from pricing. The billing model drives cash flow and is not necessarily the same as your pricing model. You may price per user per month, but then bill annually to reduce the number of transactions and sometimes to help improve cash flow.

The early entrants to the software-as-a-service model with a monthly billing model, such as Salesforce.com, had cash flow issues. When they incentivized their customers to pre-pay annually for the software in exchange for a discount, the cash flow problem was solved. A good rule of thumb is that you need about 30% of the customers to pre-pay annually to manage cash flow. Where does all the cash go? The sales and marketing process costs money, especially if the sales cycles take three to six months. You are paying sales reps during that time period, and you are not getting revenue from the customer until they buy the product.

Let's review five types of billing models and why each is utilized to meet your company and the customer's needs.

	In Arrears	Pre-Billed	Overage Billing	In App Purchases	OEM
Pros	Customers like this since they only pay for what they use.	This is great for cash flow, especially if customers pre-pay annually or even for the term of the license.	This protects your company from customers who abuse the usage model. Every software can be stretched so overage billing is used as a protection.	Creates an opportunity for customers to buy as they go and for the company to increase revenue.	This model is great as someone else is selling your software for you. You typically reduce the price by your cost of sale as the reseller bears that cost.
Cons	Is bad for cash flow as you must provide the service before you get paid.	You better not spend it all as you need this cash to operate the software!	Customers do not like this, as they cannot predict their monthly spend.	Too many in-app purchases can annoy customers, especially if everything is an in-app purchase.	To properly incent OEM software, companies sometimes pay large OEM fees, at the expense of margins

In arrears

This is also called consumption-based billing. Your utility bill works this way. You use electricity and you get a monthly bill based on how much you have used. The utility has to front the costs while you use their electricity. Hence, they sometimes charge setup or first-time connection fees to cover the float of the first month of service.

Pre-billed

Most software as a service is pre-billed now. I have seen monthly, annual, and even customers paying the entire three year term contract upfront (sometimes because they have the budget now and may not have it later).

Overage billing

Overage billing is used in conjunction with the pre-billed model to protect the software provider from customers who abuse the model. To avoid this, overage billing is added to the contract at a higher rate starting at a level which very few customers would exceed. Some companies made it their model. Cellular carriers did this early on by luring customers in with a low monthly fee, but then charged them overage fees. Beware of letting your kids watch a movie using your cellular hotspot on a road trip.

In application purchases

The gaming industry did a good job with this model. My kids asked me to buy electronic dinosaurs in the game they played. If the user had no money, like my kids, then they had to play the game longer, or watch an advertisement, to earn what they wanted. This drove up the company's ad revenue because usage time was longer. As you might expect, I was pretty annoyed by the whole situation so that is the drawback. So, be careful to not over do it.

OEM billing

This model bills your partners for software that they sold on your behalf. They are required to report on sales and pay you money based on what they have sold. It starts as an honor system, but works because customers eventually call your company for support which requires a record of the sale; so any dishonorable participants are usually caught. The customer only needs a login or install of the software, so keep track of this to manage OEM billing. This is a difficult model to set up but once it works, it is wonderful to receive checks from someone without much effort.

Licensing Models

If you are a veteran in the software industry, this will be information you are already familiar with so you may want to skip this section. New to software? Read on!

Perpetual

A perpetual licensing model is the most used by software companies until software as a service arrived ushering in subscription software. The entire cost of the software is paid upfront in the perpetual model. This is great for revenue recognition as the entire license price hits your revenue. This type of software is typically run on site (aka on premise) and conveniently can be run in isolation from others, i.e. it is not running on shared hardware.

If high performance is a must and you want control over it, this model can work well for you. There are cases where customers perpetually license software and then pay a separate hosting fee to run on someone else's hardware or cloud. So you own the software, someone else hosts it for you or provides the infrastructure for your team to then manage the software.

SAAS

The SaaS model is subscription based and is characterized by rolling the software and the cost to operate it (the hardware in infrastructure software) into one price. The margins are typically better for the selling company because one can charge more for the solution and have the customer pay for it over time. This is typical for a pay over time model. Think of a car lease versus purchasing a car and paying a monthly payment. It is better for the customer because the upfront costs are much less for them so it is easier to get the purchase done. They can also cancel after one year if the subscription term is one year. It is not as good a deal for the selling company in that the revenue is allocated over the term of the subscription.

In this model, an annual subscription of the software would be recognized monthly in your financials.

Term

Term models combine the perpetual and subscription models into a single approach. The software is managed similarly to perpetual software but the customer can only use it for the term they signed up for. The hardware and hosting costs are typically not included in a term license allowing the software to be run and managed on whatever system the customer wants.

Provisioning Model

Hybrid - this is a new model where software can run on premise, on the cloud or can easily be migrated across clouds. This type of model was enabled by solutions such as RedHat Openshift which is attempting to deliver the promise of being able to run software anywhere. This is not new by the way. The lure into Java was the same but it missed the operational side of running and managing software. So, although it delivered on being able to run the same code on multiple platforms, it missed the opportunity to deliver truly hybrid software.

Self Provisioning

Self provisioning is where a customer goes online and purchases software then the software works wherever the customer either chooses or agrees to run it. Microsoft Office Suite fits in this category. One can go online and purchase a user seat to the Microsoft Office Suite and then install it onto your desktop computer.

SaaS Provisioned

With the advent of Salesforce.com the SaaS market took its foothold as the dominant method for software to be provisioned. Under this model software runs in the cloud and is accessed online, hence the software as a service or SaaS acronym.

On Premise

The on-premise model is historically how most software was provisioned, but with the move to the cloud this is becoming more rare. In this model software is installed at the customer site on hardware that the customer purchases themselves.

Embedded

There is more and more embedded software in the market than ever before although it does not seem to get as much attention. Embedded software is implanted inside of a hardware device and is delivered along with the hardware or device. Newer products, such as the Tesla Electric Vehicle or Smart Thermostats are examples of embedded software. The Tesla can and should be viewed as a software driven solution and they were one of the first vehicle manufacturers to eliminate much of the Harvard based controls inside of a vehicle with software and sensors. Their ability to upgrade a vehicle and improve on how it operates and even adding new features by upgrading the software in the vehicle is revolutionary.

Pricing Models

Processor

This is a price per (and sometimes virtual) processor model and has become popular with infrastructure software that was charging per install. The hardware became much larger and more efficient so customers did not need as many instances (installs) of the software anymore.

User

The user pricing model is a very common approach to pricing. The price is per user of the software, but teams add in complexity by having different user types, tiers, and concurrent users, among others. Leave it to product teams to make things more complex than they need to be.

Install

The model uses the price per install of the software. For some software, user-based and install-based models become one in the same. Think of Microsoft Office where you install it locally on your computer and then pay a license fee for each install, in this case the user.

Disk space

The disk pricing model is based on the amount of disk space needed. This is often done using just the amount of disk space used and a cost per MB or TB.

Consumption based

In this model a metric is used to track the number of parts, locations, files, pictures or any other consumption-based metric and then pricing is tied to that metric. This is often done using pricing tiers. See the pricing section for more information on tiering.

So, the operating model for software is what came out of my head one late night after a disappointing week of my teams trying to work through operating models for their software solution. As tedious as it was to define each of these items, the model quickly brought clarity to my team using common terminology. I hope these explanations will bring clarity to your team as well. Architecture and Technology.

If you read through all of these your head is probably spinning. As mentioned when we started, I refer to the operating model cheat sheet myself to help guide my decision making. GTM can be complex, but breaking it down into the above models allows you to simplify it and break it down into its components. This can save weeks or even months of time. Once you choose a path, there is no reason to continue to look back unless something is not working or competition is causing you to reconsider your operating model.

DESIGN

In addition to having well-baked written requirements, the design function at my software companies has been the secret sauce for getting products to market quickly. Therefore, design output where a software developer can spend 90%+ of their time coding based on the design output, is what I define and what I have been calling, "well-baked design." Screen designs are created with such high fidelity that sometimes people do not know they are only demonstrations, even after we tell them it is a prototype. I have been doing this for 15+ years so the process is not new, but the tools have evolved. Designers used to create these designs with photoshop to make them photorealistic. Now there are tools to produce the design and generate some of the code (stylesheet/layout) resulting in the screens getting developed much faster as the developer mostly needs to then build out the back end code. These tools have enabled an amazing amount of speed in the development process. If you can pick a set of UX (user interface) controls that work out of the box without having to re-style them, even better. If you are not familiar with UX controls, items such as pull down menus, tree controls, grids, and even tooltips can be provided via code libraries to make coding go quicker. Writing these components from scratch would take a really long time.

Why do I not use developers to design screens? Would you allow a software developer to decorate your living room? I am sure there is someone out there who would say yes. But the reason I use designers is that developers tend to be left-brained and design requires an artistic element (right-brain) that is not usually found in someone who is a good coder. It turns out that I am right-brained and did not know it and is why I navigated towards being more involved in the design of the software instead of becoming a software developer. This is also the reason no one wants or would ever let me perform any coding. Would you let a software developer design or decorate your house? (please no emails from the one software developer who has designed their own house).

Most software products are built three times. The FIRST time the software is built, developers (sometimes founders) build the software without the help of designers. I can spot a software application designed by software developers a mile away. The software is functional, but the usability is poor and short cuts are made because it was the easiest way to get the software to market. Over time, customers provide feedback and the screens become even worse as they were not properly designed in the first place. Fields are added in places they do not belong causing the layouts of the screens to look even more funky. This version of the software becomes the SECOND time the software is built.

This is when it starts to look like the trailer home with 5 additions. Everyone knows it is a trailer home and can easily see what has been added on by a "do it yourself-er." The software screens become disorganized with add-ons that the software needs to be completely redesigned. This then necessitates the THIRD time the software has been built. The users of your software have been taken through this awful process and become fatigued. Their training materials match the first and second version of the software. Five years later and 20 million dollars spent, and you finally have a decent software product.

Also, with each iteration there is risk. What if the third redesign does not go well? What if users get frustrated and abandon the software during the second iteration of the software?

Therefore, the goal of well-baked or comprehensive design is to design the software correctly the First time. It requires designers and a little more time upfront, but the software development goes ridiculously faster. Do I have exact numbers on how much quicker? No. But I have watched this process over and over again and have seen how long it has taken my competitors to get products to market and know that using designers to design software is far better than using programmers to design software.

I also do not build software products three times; that wastes both time and money while increasing the risk of losing customers. During the first iteration I am working out the issues upfront by showing my high fidelity designs to customers and even potential customers, and by working out the issues on paper. Changes can be made quickly in this phase. Customers see fast results and are willing to help you make your product better as it will only benefit them. It is actually fun because you get to be part of something new and exciting.

With each iteration the software gets better and better without wasting expensive programming time and without frustrating end users with software that doesn't match their needs. Iterations of the software are then tested using RITE testing. RITE testing stands for Rapid Iterative Testing and Evaluation and is a usability testing method that focuses on identifying and resolving user interface (UI) and user experience (UX) issues in software applications. This testing approach is designed to be fast and iterative, allowing for rapid cycles of testing and refinement.

RITE testing involves the following steps:

1. Preparation
2. Testing
3. Observation and Feedback
4. Debriefing
5. Rinse and Repeat

Preparation

In this phase, the testing team defines the goals and objectives of the testing, identifies target users (personas), and sets up the testing method (we do most of our testing over Zoom style meetings recording the sessions). The team designs test scenarios and tasks that users will perform during testing.

Testing

During the testing phase, participants are asked to perform specific tasks using the software being tested. They are often observed by usability experts, designers, and the product team. The testing process emphasizes real-time observation and feedback collection. The information you receive is invaluable. We typically test three to five users. There tends to be a diminishing return on the number of people as they start repeating the same things. Users are also time-consuming to recruit and you will want to do more rounds of testing.

Ideally you use "fresh" users every time. Researchers are trained to get users to think aloud, not answering questions for them, making them provide what they "think" the screen is supposed to do.

Observation and Feedback

Observers watch and take notes as participants interact with the software. Some of the observers are watching a recording of the session as you do not want to pile on too many observers when there is only one user on the other end providing feedback. Observers pay attention to usability issues, user confusion, assess where they are having difficulties in completing tasks, and any unexpected behavior. Feedback from both participants and observers is collected during or immediately after each testing session.

Debriefing

After each RITE iteration, the testing team holds a debriefing session. The findings and observations are discussed and analyzed. Usability issues are categorized based on their severity and impact on the user experience.

Refinement: Based on the issues identified during testing, the design team (and sometimes the development) team makes quick, iterative changes to the UI/UX (user interface / user experience) design.

These changes address usability problems discovered during the RITE testing and improve the overall user experience.

Rinse and Repeat: The "improved" design is subjected to further RITE testing sessions and the cycle continues until the usability issues are minimized and the user experience meets the desired standards. There is typically a diminishing return after two to three cycles unless there are major issues with the design. Be ready to do as many iterations as needed to get it right.

There are other testing approaches, but RITE testing has some distinct advantages. The first advantage is the rapid identification of issues. The iterative nature of RITE testing allows for quick identification of usability issues. The process is interactive, meaning issues are fixed and then further testing is conducted, resulting in further improvements to the product. This allows you to "fully cook" your solutions. Observing users and collecting feedback in real-time provides immediate insights into how they interact with the interface, leading to a more accurate assessment of user behaviors.

Plus, the improvements are iterative and adapt easily to an Agile development approach. The back-and-forth process of testing and refinement leads to incremental improvements in the interface, taking it through the iterations that typically happen over that three-to-five-year timeframe in just a few weeks. This results in a more user-friendly and efficient product built correctly the first time.

RITE testing may not cover all types of usability issues and is not as comprehensive as other more formal testing methods. but it has produced great results for me, saving both money and time in the long run.

The Design "Team"

It turns out that you just can't use a single designer to produce a good result. Design is made up of four separate skills that include interaction design, graphic design, visual design, and research. This requires a combination of people, some of which are only needed part-time. For example, the visual designer will help pick the color scheme of the software, but once it is set, only adjustments are needed from time to time.

Interaction Designer

This designer is a master at laying out the overall navigational structure of your software and the overall screen flow. Think of them as an information architect for screens. They do the bulk of the screen design. This is often a full-time role during the life of the project.

Graphic Designer

A graphic designer is used to design graphics and things like icons in software. This is sometimes detailed work using graphics tools that take time to master. Not taking the time to design graphics properly can negate the time you spend making the interactions of the software amazing. This is typically a part-time role (unless the product is extremely large). It is likely that generative AI will revolutionize the graphic design industry, providing better tools to make generating high quality graphics much faster.

Visual Designer

As stated above, visual designers make the screens pretty. They pick the right colors, spacing, and help fix any issues while providing an overall great experience with the product. Sometimes just improving the visual design helps improve software sales. This role is also typically part-time.

Researcher

A researcher performs RITE studies to ensure that the designs are usable with a high level of discoverability, which is the bulk of the research work. Someone well-trained in how to perform user research will pay high dividends during the design cycle. Watching a researcher for the first time with a user is frustrating.

They avoid telling the user what to do if they are stuck, but it is how they get users to "think out loud." Let them do their job. In some projects, researchers also do generative research, which mean they help you determine what the market and users need when you are not 100% sure what product to build. I typically know the market where I am launching software, but I have still leveraged researchers to see if they can "dig up" some insights my team may have missed. I consider this R&D as I may or may not get a return on this investment.

Who not to hire!

Do not be fooled by someone who has been designing websites and thinks they can design enterprise software. If your software is a website, then by all means hire a web designer. Enterprise software requires a different set of skills and a different way of thinking. The way you design interactions and layout screens is very different for enterprise software than it is for websites. For one thing, the padding on websites spaces everything out because you are trying to feed users information as they scroll down your screen and one can only consume so much information at once in this scrollable world. In enterprise software, you are oftentimes trying to do the opposite. You want to show everything on one screen to prevent scrolling whenever possible. Designers who understand enterprise software are much harder to find than web designers, but their skills are invaluable. Take the time to find the right resource who understands how enterprise software is used and built.

Wireframes vs High Fidelity

Sometimes wireframes (or even sketches) are used to work through the basic flow of the screens. If you do not have the interaction design and basic screen flow worked out using wireframes or sketches can save time. High fidelity screens are more time-consuming to produce. In the end, you should still create high fidelity designs, but starting with wire frames can help you work through conceptually what you want the software to do. Tools like Figma.com are now used to produce high fidelity screens that look and act like real software.

Personas

A user persona (Veal, 2023) is a fictional representation of a user group that helps designers and developers understand the needs, goals, and behaviors of their target audience User personas are created based on data collected from interviews, surveys, and other research methods. They typically include demographic information, such as age, gender, education level, and occupation, as well as psychographic information, such as interests, values, and personality traits.

Download Example Software User Personas

Design Patterns

For larger software organizations, I would highly recommend using a design system and leveraging design patterns. Designing ineffectively looks like five different teams designing dashboard screens in five different software products, all re-inventing the wheel. Your software products will also look like they came from five different companies. This does not bode well when you are in larger deals trying to sell customers multiple products from your company. Sometimes products are acquired so they inevitably will look different, but if you never start working on patterns, then you will never finish, so you might as well start today. This enables your product to scale and you will see the productivity of your design team increase by an order of magnitude. Designers across your entire organization can provide input into the patterns so they will improve over time. Some steps involved in creating a design system:

1. Assemble your best team
2. Define the "superset" of screen patterns needed (you are looking for the highest potential coverage across all of your screens)
3. Create written requirements for the screen patterns needed in your design system
4. Create generalized requirements for areas such as accessibility, form factor (mobile, tablet, laptop), etc.
5. Define your overall visual design (look and feel, colors)
6. Start with the header, footer and navigation
7. Prioritize design for patterns in the design system
8. Design patterns
9. Perform user testing (RITE studies) on the patterns
10. Obtain feedback from consumers of the patterns
11. Pick controls that meet your requirements and design; you may have to adjust designs and requirements, unless you have unlimited time and money.

Similar to design patterns, you can turn design patterns into code by building standardized components or choose open source or licensed UI controls that meet the requirements in the pattern. Developers can then quickly import code patterns that match your company's design patterns. Building controls can be complex and time-consuming, so I am typically looking for widely used and well-tested controls. This then speeds up software development by an order of magnitude. On one software product, we went through three different grid controls. The first one looked cool because it was using Ajax to dynamically load data. Ajax was also new and the developers wanted to use it. It turns out the control was trying to download all of the data to the browser. That was fine until we had tables with millions of rows and the browser would run out of memory. The next grid control turned out to be buggy. It had all of the features we needed but the team was forever trying to find bugs in this control as they did not pay attention to the "widely used" rule I had given them. The third control, widely used, worked great but we had to modify it as it also ran into issues once the grid had millions of records, but with some minor modifications, it served us well for the next 10 years. Each iteration burned 8-10 weeks of developer time. I now require my teams to run a "spike" on new controls, loading tables with lots of data, seeing how they work with low bandwidth browser connections, making sure they support translations, among other things.

Tiger teams

A tiger team is a group of specialists who purposely and creatively solve a problem (*Tiger Team*, Wikipedia). I have used tiger teams to create step-change improvements in product design to solve complex problems. The best known example is during the Apollo 13 mission in 1970 (Williams, 2021). A team of specialists was formed to address the problems that arose when part of the Apollo 13 service module malfunctioned and exploded.

Have a complex problem to solve? Form a tiger team and let them be creative, removing the typical barriers to moving a product forward. You may produce a result that seemed unachievable. For example, Sophia Levins, while at IBM, ran tiger teams for a new supply chain product I was launching. The tiger team consisted of people from design, product and development and was tasked with quickly prototyping new solutions. This approach, although produced some throw-away work, also accelerated the overall thinking of the entire team. It also helped bring along the entire team as there were varying levels of understanding as to what would be needed to get a supply chain product to market. As Sophia ran subsequent iterations, the tiger team became a lion team and then a bear team for each major design cycle.

Sustainable design

A more recent trend is designing to reduce the energy usage of the software. This typically involves reducing the image sizes on the screen and reducing the amount of data that has to be read and written to the database. Transmitting data and reading/writing data consumes energy. Reducing the computational intensity of software also reduces energy consumption, but may be more difficult to achieve by making changes to the user interface, but not impossible. My first reaction to sustainable design was that I thought my teams were doing this all along. Isn't this just good design? Smaller images and less data makes the screens draw faster and more efficiently. It is possible that I am just old and grew up in an era where computers had very little disk space and memory so you optimized everything. That being said, being sustainable seems to motivate my teams more than creating performant screens as they seemed to only pay attention to energy use if there was a problem (i.e. a screen was slow). A really good reference is IBM's design for sustainability white paper which can be found here:

Takeaways:

- Perform RITE testing and avoid building and (re)designing your product 3 times.
- Hire the right people with experience in enterprise software design.
- Leverage design patterns where possible.
- Periodically leverage Tiger teams to accelerate innovation.
- Turn designs into code leveraging an intentionally chosen set of UI controls.

SOFTWARE DEVELOPMENT

I am going to cover five topics in software development. There is so much written about how to code, how to manage development teams, and technology topics yet there are four areas that are less-often discussed but more important. This includes:

- developer talent
- technology stack
- joint development
- open source software
- engaging developers

Your single most important item to get right in software development is the talent you hire to build your product. Although I use some contractors, one cannot outsource the development of your software when you are a software company (and still be considered a software company in my mind). I have learned there are four different outcomes from a coding task based on which software developer you hired.

Outcome 1 - The coding task is completed in one day.

Outcome 2 - The coding task is completed in two (to three) days.

Outcome 3 - The coding task is completed in 5-10 days (most likely 10).

Outcome 4 - The code base is damaged, slowing down outcome 1, 2 or 3.

GIven the amount of time ranges from 1 to ten days (excluding outcome 4), you could hire one developer capable of outcome 1 and achieve the work of 10 developers. Now hire a team of developers in the Outcome 1 and 2 category, and you can achieve the same as fifty to one hundred outcome 3 software developers. This drove me to become fanatical about how to hire software developers. This often involves giving them a coding task with a limited timeframe and then jointly walking through their code with them, asking them questions about why they did what they did in the code. You are better off with less developers but higher calibur as they will outperform larger teams. These developers are going to cost you more, but the differential more than makes up for the difference.

A technology stack is the set of technologies used to build your software. For example, as I am writing this a common technology stack would consist of Java, React, Node.js, and a database such as PostGreSQL among other things. To bring what a technology stack is to light, here is an example of the technology stack for one of the products I launched:

Very little software today is written from scratch as it would take too long. When picking the technology stack for a software product, think "widely used and stable." The rule I give to developers is, I do not want any version 1.0 components in my software. The same applies to the "latest and greatest" version of anything. It is more efficient to stay one version back.

Despite best efforts, even widely used software does not eliminate hard-to-find issues. We were using Xerces for XML transactions in a software solution; it was widely used by 1000's of companies for almost five years at that point in time. I was getting support tickets from customers that we were losing transactions. It turned out that I was losing about 1 in every 5000 transactions. Finding this was a needle in the haystack sort of problem. It was not 1.0 software, it was widely used. Has anyone not used it at the same volumes that we were? Possibly not, we were pushing the limits of this software. It only goes downhill from here as you get closer to 1.0 software and software that has not been battle tested. Let competitors debug the latest release, wait up to six months to upgrade. Your customer just wants software that works. They do not care if you use the newest release of an open source component. After months of difficult customer calls and an inordinate amount of time spent on the issue from my software development team, a developer named Joseph, who walked around the office barefoot, found the issue. There was what is called a threading (or race condition) in the Xerces library. Because of the type of issue and because it was in a third party library, finding the issues was extremely difficult. This becomes tricky when trying to keep up to date with security patches. Some open source and third party components have the ability to patch only security-related fixes. The argument is that you have to keep software up to date to ensure the latest security patches have been applied. This is not always true. In one recent example, the latest version of Log4J had a security flaw that allowed systems to be hacked. Bad actors are working harder than ever to embed trojan horses inside widely used open source. The companies that were running a later release of log4j avoided having a security flaw in their software.

I have yet to manage a software product where we did not get something wrong. It is inevitable and realize that it is part of the process. I have learned that if a technology is causing major problems or requires the company to take a risk that is not worth it, the sooner we admit we made a bad decision and fix it the better off we were. Allocate a sprint or two to fixing technical debt and allow the team to move forward in a better way. Realize that even the best teams are not 100% perfect. Don't worry, it happens.

In addition to picking the right technology stack your team should document it. I always have a one-paged picture of your technology stack so that everyone is on the same page. This seems simple, but I have asked software teams for their stack and was told they would get back to me in two weeks. Seriously? In the go-to-market deliverables section of this book there is a technology overview presentation that is needed by sales in order to deal with questions from company IT departments, so you need this anyway.

You do not want your technology stack, meaning the technologies you have used in your software, to be out of control. You must have a single throat to choke on technology architecture decisions. If that person is spineless or makes bad decisions, you are in trouble. A CTO who does not pay attention to what stack decisions are being made is not really in charge. There are plenty out there. They may be smart, know a lot about the technology, love to spend time with the team bantering about what technologies to use, but have no idea what developers are reviewing in the code.

One software offering had twelve (12) different technologies for the user interface. Another offering had four different grid controls, all with different looks and feels, capabilities, multiple database technologies and experimented with a new way to store data. The result was not desirable for anyone involved; the customer, the developers, support and even partners were impacted. It was difficult to apply fixes, make improvements, and in general, a challenge to move the customers and the offering forward. Streamline your process, select an architecture type and move forward. Don't allow portions of your business to linger because no one is willing to cut out the less-than-great parts that will distract, draw resources and ultimately hold back your team and your customers' success.

Another common mistake is going to market with proprietary technology and architecture when a product does not warrant it. There are instances where proprietary technology is warranted but for most software products you can get to market much quicker by assembling existing open source or licensed software that is embedded in your solution. Customers primarily care that the solution works and is secure, not that you created your own programming language and are smart. Your competitors will run circles around you while you are building the Taj Mahal of software. Others will snatch up market share from under your nose because they can get to market much quicker by not reinventing the wheel. Creativity doesn't always mean creating something from scratch but can encompass putting together items that already exist in a unique way. Take for example what Apple did with iTunes (now the apple music store). The MP3 player already existed. There were platforms to download software (Napster.) There were online stores. Apple put all three together into one single seamless solution and the rest was history, forever changing the music industry.

If your software requires proprietary technology, then proceed with caution. Sometimes it is inevitable, you are charting waters that have never been swum in before. Just know where the sharks are.

Over the years, I have engaged in jointly building out solutions with customers. This is sometimes initiated by the customers as they have a high value business need and there is no software on the market that meets their needs. This can work out well for both parties as long as both the scope and timelines are managed properly. Projects where the person or team interfacing with the customer does not have the capacity to say no will result in projects that either never finish, have significant time and cost overruns, or result in an extremely unhappy customer or even worse, all of these items at once. Setting a clear joint development agreement and methodology to guide the process is key. I would have executive-level meetings monthly with the customer to ensure blockers on both your and their end are quickly resolved. For the direct team, they should be on daily or minimally weekly playbacks reviewing requirements, design and working code. The customer becomes part of your team in a true agile-oriented joint-development sprint plan.

A significant amount of commercial software is built upon open-source solutions. Pay attention to the type of open source agreements your team uses as some require you to open source your entire solution if you embed theirs. Your company should have a vetting process for any new component embedded in your software and a bill of materials for all open source components. There are solutions that can help you keep track of and manage components. If you ever plan to sell your company, the buyer will scan your entire codebase for open source licensing to ensure you have properly licensed all embedded components that require a license. I would not cut corners on any of this. Once again, I am not a lawyer and would therefore leverage one to train your team periodically on what to pay attention to as the laws can change over time.

I do not believe software developers are being engaged enough. I make them show up to a bi-weekly sprint playback meeting and make them demo their work. Most enjoy this as they have worked hard on it. I will sit with them, even as a CEO, and drill them with questions. I learn something new every time I do this and the software developer does too. I also have sent developers into power plants, manufacturing facilities, and call centers, to visit train stations and bridges. Sometimes for months at a time. Having them sit right next to the users of the software helps them better understand what they are building and how it is used. On one software product, we had closed our first large deal and on a site visit, we learned that the customer was planning to roll out the software to hundreds of users within the next few weeks. This was great, except that we had not fully load-tested this software. If we had not visited the site we would not have known this. Our sales team certainly did not think to tell anyone. We promptly kicked off load testing and their implementation was a success.

Takeaways:

- Hire the best talent you can afford. Less is better.
- Pick the right technology stack using someone who is qualified to pick the technologies in your stack.
- Combining existing code, controls and frameworks is a faster path to market than writing everything from scratch.
- Joint development with customers can be beneficial if properly managed.
- Stick with proven, stable technologies.
- Leverage opens source, but pay attention to open source licensing.
- Fully engage your software developers and immerse them in the problem.

Artifacts:

QR Code - Example technology stack, technology overview, joint development methodology, joint development agreement.

Download Example Technology Stack

Download Example Technology Overview

Download Joint Development Methodology

SALES

There is a lot that could be said about sales, but I am going to focus on a few areas that are the most critical:

- The demo
- The value process
- Sales talent
- Install base sales
- Sales operations

The Demo

During a sales demo what I am looking for are customers jumping out of their seats excited about my solution. They are finishing our sentences and talking about how the software could work at their company. They are envisioning their people using the solution. They are also paying attention during the demo, not looking at their phones or doing other things. If this is not happening, you have an issue with either your demo or your messaging. Go fix it.

Become a master of body language if you want to know what to do next in a demo. I was on a sales call and my sales rep after the meeting exclaimed about how the deal was almost done. I asked him "why do you think that?" He gave me the typical response that the demo went well, it is a solution they needed and they were discussing implementation. I told him there was no way they were going to buy this software in the next six months. He was a bit confused and asked me to explain. I had been watching the body language of the executive in the room who had to approve the budget for our software. She was fidgety and looked very nervous. During a break mid-way in the demo, I followed her out to grab coffee and asked her if there was anything holding her back from buying the software. She seemed relieved to tell me, in confidence, that they did not have the budget to buy the software even though her team is excited by the capabilities in our solution. If I had paid attention to my rep, I would be wondering why at the end of my quarter I missed my numbers. Instead, I read the room and my forecast was accurate. They eventually bought the software, but in the next fiscal year.

One additional point on sales demos that may result in me getting some nasty emails is, don't worry, I don't actually read them. Your sales reps should be able to demo your software. No matter how large the company. I disagree with the view that sales reps should not know all the features of your product to eliminate the chance of a feature war with competitors or amongst internal teams. I take a different approach.

A sales rep who cannot answer basic questions about a company's products has nothing to sell besides their charming personality. Well-trained reps are also typically smart enough to avoid a feature war and should be equipped to answer product questions when pressed.

The Value Process

Have a prescribed method for guiding the customer down the path to see the value in your software in comparison to what they pay for it. If the value they see is not greater than the purchase price, they will not buy the software. If they have no context for where to associate value, they will not purchase the software. If your sales are product-led, you have minutes to achieve this. If you have a traditional sales process, you have more time but are always better off getting to value as soon as you can in the process. For more traditional sales, a value calculator is a best practice. This is an exercise you engage in jointly with your customer to calculate the value they would achieve. You accomplish this using your value calculator with their data. In the end, they have to believe in what the value calculator is implying, but given it is their data, this is oftentimes easy to do. They would not engage in this level of detail if they did not see "some" value in your software. At one software company we would charge for this process because the value assessment alone delivered value to the customer, even if they did not purchase our software. We measured that if a customer engaged with us in a value assessment, about 75% of the time they purchased the software, increasing the probability from 20%.

Sales Talent

Generally, with sales talent you get what you pay for. Experienced sales reps are coin-operated: they can generate significant income if they work at the right company with the right products and, of course, if they are assigned to the right accounts that can bring in a lot of revenue. There were some years where my top salesperson made more than me, the CEO of the company. As a CEO, this was worth it as revenue is the lifeblood of a company. The revenue for many software businesses is recurring.

If the seller sells a one or three-year subscription and I pay commission on that duration, but the customer winds up using the software for 10-15 years, it's worth it! In this type of software and GTM model, there is typically an attainment or level of new revenue a salesperson will bring in per year. Therefore, it is always a good idea to speak to some experienced sales leaders or CEOs of companies that sell software to understand how much revenue a salesperson should be closing per year. Typically, your top salesperson will sell two times more than what your average rep sells.

To avoid enabling sellers to collect deals as they come in without any effort, you need to have an established process in place that is clearly communicated to your sales personnel. For example, a company that achieves a certain level of brand recognition will get deals coming in regardless of whether a sales rep makes a single cold call. It is not a good use of the company capital to build an order-taking operation using expensive sales representatives versus building a sales force that has to sell to add a significant amount of value. This does not mean that you shouldn't hand inbound leads to sellers. Instead, spread out inbound leads requiring all sellers to work their way into a new white space account. A white space account is a new customer, sometimes called a "logo," where the selling company does not yet have revenue. Give sellers a challenge! Both you and your salespeople will be better off. Sellers should be selling into accounts that the company would not have otherwise closed. We will go into establishing commission plans later.

There are two types of sales personnel, hunters and farmers. During the interview process every seller claims they are a hunter (as opposed to a farmer). This term is widely used to describe a seller who goes out and finds customers vs sitting on existing customers and driving more revenue. In a software company of modest size, there is a role for both types of sellers and they require very different skill sets.

I have found that most reps are not actually hunters. Don't get me wrong, many of these sales reps *are* capable of being a hunter, but I have also observed that no grown man or woman likes to get to get the phone hung up on them. As reps progress in their career, they are more likely to get burned out on this type of selling. To get around this I have hired companies to do the prospecting and then hand the leads to my reps. Calling fifty or one hundred companies a day is a high burn-out position and it is best to leave this type of work to someone who has the expectation that they are going to make this many calls, emails, or reach outs via LinkedIn.

To better focus hunter vs farmer skills, in more than one company, I split the sellers into reps who manage and sell to the install base (current customers) and sellers who go and find new customers. The sellers are focused on one or the other based on their skillset. For example, a software company that has not added a lot of new logos in a long time may require that you hire sellers who are better suited towards hunting. Why? Because your history suggests your team is most likely made up of gatherers.

I have also seen more than one software company that had reps handling both new logo sales and playing the role of an account manager for an existing customer even though they have very different skill sets. If the rep is a strong seller and assigned to an existing customer that has little opportunity for sales growth, there is a tendency for customers to be annoyed as they are looking for someone to help improve their business using your software they already have. Meanwhile, your sales rep is just trying to sell them *more* software. The goals are not aligned.

I have had customers thank me when I removed a seller from their account. At first, I thought that I had a bad seller on my hands, but I learned that was not always the case. In one instance, I had sellers locked into a single account with a quota that was not attainable based on what this customer needed. The sellers were trying desperately to meet quotas but it was a losing battle.

On the other hand, a sales representative who is a strong account manager (farmer) can produce low or even zero attainment if given a bunch of new customers to call on. This same representative will produce amazing results on install base accounts where a farmer has plenty of fertile soil to till.

Additionally, be careful to work out the gray areas. For example, you do not want to penalize a sales representative for closing an initial deal just to have the remaining account value get taken away and given to an install base sales representative when they are not really finished closing the account. Decide when to transition.

Install Base Sales

Now, what about those loyal customers? Selling into the existing customer (install) base is often overlooked. At one company, we grew sales by over 25% in one year by setting up a dedicated team to sell only to existing customers. We created a new organization called Customer Success who was commissioned to help the customer achieve success. These individuals were knowledge experts on both the customer's business and the software. They were extremely helpful in identifying ways the customer could achieve greater success using our software products.

At one software company, I established this organization from the ground up and saw sales increase by over 20% almost exclusively driven by install-base sales generated by this newly created organization. What they were selling was very different from what the reps had previously been trying to sell. The prior reps were pushing the customer base to purchase new licenses. Then the customer success organization I established started selling training, helped configuring the system, paid assessments to determine how customers could get more value out of the software, accelerated features, building custom reports, etc. The deal sizes were much smaller and tended to be services, but the revenue added up and customers were much happier. Subsequently, customers expanded the use of the software and increased license purchases now that they finally achieved success using the software we had already sold them.

Now, sales mean commissions. Commission plans are always a challenging aspect of managing a sales or customer success organization. Most companies make them more complex than they need to be. I have even seen more than one software company not put its commission plan in writing, which is ripe for all sorts of issues, including legal issues. Do not create/offer a commission plan via email or a verbal conversation.

At one company I took over, I finally sent an email to the entire sales team stating that "If anyone had anything else promised to them by the prior CEO, they had ten days to come forward with some proof of this agreement in writing, otherwise, there will be no more discussions about what the prior CEO had promised." Sales commissions should be well documented, and sales reps should not be subjected to constantly changing sales plans. Change the plan when the objectives or GTM strategy of the company changes.

This should not even have to be said, but if a sales rep makes a large commission, pay it. At one large software company, a sales rep closed a $100 million dollar deal and the company later refused to pay the commission because the CEO thought it was too large of a sum to pay a sales rep. This sales rep sued the company and won. In the end it was not worth both the legal fees nor the reputation damage this software company brought upon themselves. Who would want to work for that software company?

Install base sales (or sometimes called customer success) should work on commission but on a different structure. They should be selling things that help the customer be successful, such as training, smaller service deals designed to help the customer achieve goals. Minimally, if the revenue from these sales pays for the customer success team it is worth it. In reality, I have seen these reps bring in significant revenue. In one case, I increased the overall revenues of the company by 20% by creating a customer success team where none had existed. No one was helping the install base be successful. These companies had money and were willing to pay for additional help. They rewarded the company by expanding the use of their software to more locations, divisions, and regions across the globe. They also started providing references.

Sales Operations

Now, let's talk about the operational side of selling. It is surprising how many software companies do not have a well-defined sales process. If you are just getting your business started I would leverage the simple model of tracking leads, opportunities, wins, lost deals and disqualified leads. Oftentimes, the sales process is more sophisticated than this, but one has to start somewhere. The sales and marketing process moves potential customers one at a time from one stage to the next and hence closer to becoming a customer of your software. There should be a clear list of prospective customers on which both marketing and sales are aligned.

A company should know who their next 100, 250, or 1000 customers are by name. This list is the "leads." Once the customer is reached and it appears that there is a qualified need for your software, the lead moves into the opportunity stage. There should be clear qualification criteria before a lead becomes an opportunity, otherwise, your sales opportunity (a.k.a. your pipeline) will be overstated. Metrics on how many customers have progressed should be reviewed minimally at least monthly. Weekly or biweekly is even better. Below is an example of how pipeline progression was measured at one of the software companies I ran. Lack of progress means that there is 1) a product problem, 2) an issue with messaging, or 3) the sales representative and/or process is ineffective. The monthly numbers are the number achieved that month, not a cumulative total.

YTD	Jan	Feb	Mar	Apr	May	Jun	Jul	Aug	Sep	Oct	Nov	Dec	Total
Leads	250	250	253	255	255	255	258	258	258	258	258	258	**258**
Opportunity	16	6	7	13	4	6	4	14	10	3	8	2	**93**
Won	0	2	2	1	4	2	0	1	1	1	0	0	**14**
Lost	0	1	0	2	3	3	4	5	5	5	6	7	**0**
Disqualified	0	3	5	10	11	15	18	22	25	30	33	35	**35**

These metrics can be tracked on a cumulative basis or you can track net new leads, opportunities, etc. or both. I like to see the cumulative progression starting with a list of who I think my target customers are. This gives me clear visibility of whether or not I am reaching and converting them to be my customers. Tracking metrics by campaign stage will be covered in more detail in the marketing chapter of this book.

I cannot overemphasize the importance of enabling your sales reps. I have used: a one-pager approach and role playing techniques while pitching the level one deck, shadowing other sales reps, and having them sit through product training courses. Having a value calculator and making sure reps understand the value drivers customers are using to make buying decisions is critical. A rep should understand the ins and outs of your product and both the buying and user personas for your product.

Sales is the lifeblood of your company. Therefore, go out and find the best sales talent you can afford, enable them with great demos, value calculators, and the GTM materials (described in the chapter on go-to-market) that make your company and products look like they are worth it.

Artifacts:

Download Metrics Tracking Template

Download Sales Process

Download Seller 1-Pager

Download Example Value Calculator

Takeaways

- Learn how to read the room in a sales demo. This can be accomplished even online.
- Invest in a value assessment calculator and process.
- Think through how to manage your install base (aka existing customers) versus new account sales.
- Have clear sales commission plans and keep them simple.
- Incent customer success teams that align the customer's goals with your team's sales goals.
- Know where sales opportunities are in the pipeline via sales metrics.
- Invest in external BDR to make the cold calls.
- Invest in seller training, ideally an in-person annual sales kick off and either monthly or quarterly online sales updates.

MARKETING

I was early in the launch of a business, a combined software and marketing agency, and I tend to get wrapped up in my launch working long hours so I decided to see what was going on in Austin. I tend to work on one launch and then directly launch another, rarely coming up for air. This was one of the times I needed some air. The early part of the launch cycle of a business involves long hours. It can be isolating, so every once in a while, I want to get out of the office to do something extraordinary. This time I signed up for a free seminar with Gary Keller of Keller Williams.

He showed up wearing a black short sleeve shirt and black jeans and seemed like the type of guy who did not really care what anyone thought of him. He sat at the front of the room with an overhead foil projector. Anyone born in 1980 or later has no idea what this is. Basically, you write on transparent film with different color markers and it projects what you are writing on the wall. Of course, Gary used only a black marker. This is how things were done before today's projectors or fancy TV screens were invented. I was amused that he was still using one.

Gary made a point that I will never forget. He said in any business you need to keep segmenting the market until you become the leader in something. It may be a tiny slice, but you are the leader. From there you can make decisions to go horizontally or vertically, but you at least have a starting point. This is sound advice and I have used it over and over. To win, you have to have some sort of differentiation and better messaging.

For messaging, Gary Schwake from the Yield Group has some great advice, "simplify messaging: It is easy to talk about your killer product, high-quality services and unmatched internal support, but none of that is actually relevant to your customers. They don't care about you, they care about solving their problems. Great product marketing explains what your product does and how it helps your customers. No jargon, no buzzwords." This approach provides a perspective that makes spending countless hours on your logo seem silly, as customers don't care what your logo looks like unless it is weird.

In terms of differentiation, ideally it is a corner of the market you have captured leading to rampant success for those customers. It does not always need to have more features than the competitor. I have won in markets where I had new software and a lot less features than my competitor. How did I do this? Well, my competitor was on an older software architecture and in this instance, companies wanted to move towards SaaS-based solutions. Companies were willing to accept fewer features in software that was easier to use and that they did not have to directly manage themselves. PC based software managed across 100+ sites was costing this company a lot of money. Employees were working from home and their helpdesk did not know how to help someone debug software running on a PC. By providing some key features the customer needed that my competitor did not have, I was able to gain market share even though my product was not yet as robust as the competition's product. As much as possible, choose a feature that would be very difficult for the competition to implement without a major overhaul of their software. This way you become the leader in this area.

We've touched on a few of these marketing methods previously, but it's important to remember that your techniques will vary depending upon your GTM strategy being product-led or sales-led. If you recall, under the product-led model, the marketing is geared towards getting customers to sign up for your solution online. This means the customer needs enough information about your product to make a purchasing decision immediately. The price point for the software also needs to be low enough for a customer to use either a personal or corporate credit card. In product-led marketing, the marketing does not stop after the customer purchases the product. The initially low price point usually means there is an attempt to upsell the customer after the initial purchase. If there is a low retention rate after the initial sign up there will also be work required after the initial purchase.

Sales-led and product-led marketing are incompatible so you need to define clear lanes if both are to exist within a company. For example, with P6 Technologies we are leading with a product-led approach and then once several individuals in a company purchase the software an enterprise sales rep will call the account to determine if there is an opportunity to sell an enterprise-wide license. In a sales-led model the goal is to schedule an appointment between a prospective customer and one of your sales reps or to give your sales rep a reason to follow up with a customer to have a conversation. For example, a customer downloading a white paper (or other gated assets) can trigger a sales rep to call a prospective customer.

Regardless of whether a product-led or sales-led approach is used a company needs to have a list of who it thinks are its next 50, 250, and 1000 customers. I joke around with my team and tell them they also need to know the color of their contact's eyes. If you do not know who they are there is a very low chance they will become your customer anytime soon. The model of spending massive amounts of money on branding style advertising is dead unless you are a very large corporation with a massive advertising budget.

Given that most companies do not have massive marketing budgets, a more targeted account-based approach is significantly more cost effective. If you know who your next 50 customers should be, then you really just need to call, email them, or if your software is network-based, someone needs to invite them. It seriously is not any more complicated than that. Now, do not get me wrong, it is hard to reach customers and if you approach them with the wrong messaging, you are dead in the water. It is worth the time and effort to tune your messaging before making calls. Do some trials first to see if customers respond.

Product Pages

It's not only about calling your potential customers as we've seen with product and sales-led marketing approaches. Unfortunately, most software companies have horrible websites and even worse product pages. They seem to get worse over time. If a company has only one product, then the entire website should be a product page. The following is a good guideline of what a great product page should have:

1. A very clear statement at the top of the page telling what the product does.
2. A hook.
3. Some eye candy to make the product look amazing.
4. Customer testimonials and/or logos.
5. Validation from analysts.
6. Pricing (if product-led).
7. A clear value statement.
8. The ability to chat with someone (if you have the resources).
9. Answers to typical questions needed to make a buying decision (for example, if integration is always a question then a list of or link to a page with all of your amazing integrations would be appropriate).
10. Lead magnets (white papers, webinars, trials or other helpful information).

Marketing Coordination

Many software organizations lack general coordination between the product, partner, sales, and marketing teams. Lack of coordination is expected in a large company, but this applies to smaller startups as well. Ask any startup CEO when their website messaging, product pages, or scheduled events have been updated and they are caught off-guard in front of a major customer who is asking about the specific change. You can't see me, but my hand is raised. To avoid this, I now have my marketing team keep a simple marketing calendar to let everyone know what is happening and when, including me. This sounds too simple, but I have received pushback from marketing on their team being open and transparent as to what is happening when.

Marketing Calendar

	Jan	Feb	Mar	Apr	May	Jun	Jul	Aug	Sep	Oct	Nov	Dec
Message Development	Vision	Refine										
Build Maintenance/Reliability List	✓	✓										
Influencer Campaign	Build List	Build List	Build List	Build List								
Account-Based Marketing (ABM) Program	Identify Prospects	Identify Prospects	Identify Prospects	Identify Prospects			Execute	Execute	Execute	Execute	Execute	Execute
New Web Site Design	Finalize	Implement										
Google AdWords/Remarketing		✓	✓	✓	✓	✓	✓	✓	✓	✓	✓	✓
Sales Collateral					Create Content	Create Content/Execute						
Press Releases			As Needed	As Needed	As Needed	As Needed	As Needed	As Needed	As Needed	As Needed	As Needed	As Needed
Update Trade Show Banners		✓	✓	✓	✓	✓						
Customer Days Planning												
Events												
Business Development Leads		✓	✓	✓	✓	✓	✓	✓	✓	✓		✓
Product Launch Comms			✓	✓	✓	✓			✓	✓	✓	
White Papers		✓		✓								
LinkedIn Campaigns			✓	✓	✓	✓	✓	✓	✓	✓	✓	
Videos												

A necessary evil in today's noisy world is digital advertising. The rate of return on the investment can be very low with this type of advertising. If mis-managed, your "ad spend" may report high numbers, but if you are not getting conversions to sales then they are fooling you by sending the wrong traffic to the site. The reason: to either make the numbers look higher or your site/messaging is broken. You can burn months trying to fix this. Sometimes it may be better to run tests with landing pages and move the traffic off of your website. If you are not familiar, a landing page is a temporary page set up specifically for a marketing campaign. Oftentimes, these are hosted on third-party sites but it is better to build and host them on your own website if you can. You can quickly implement multiple landing pages and see how they convert to actual sales. There are now some AI-driven platforms that are interesting, modeling your best google analytics expert, but operating on more information than a single person could manage.

Marketing automation if done properly helps a very small marketing team scale. For example, a customer visits your website and downloads a white paper. Because they opted in to receiving information from your company, your marketing automation platform can then notify a sales rep to book an appointment with that customer in two weeks to ask what they thought about the white paper. The automation platform can also kick off a series of helpful emails giving the prospect relevant and useful industry information. And it can then automatically invite them to attend the next webinar or local meet up organized by you or one of your partners. All this with little to no interaction with your marketing team.

This brings up email marketing. This, unfortunately, has gotten more difficult with spam filters in the US and privacy laws in Europe such as GDPR. If you do not know about GDPR, look up the billions of dollars in fines companies like Facebook have received. Wind up on a spam list and it could take a lot of work to get your URL removed. For me this causes stress I do not need. Using an account-based approach, it is often better to send personalized emails or try to reach the potential customer via LinkedIn, than to risk being labeled a spammer. I know there will be people out there who will argue with me on this topic, but I personally have not had great results from email marketing unless the list of customers are just that, my existing customers who recognize my brand and want to hear from me (most of the time).

I am a big fan of remarketing once you ensure the right customers are connecting to your website. I describe remarketing as "following" a user around after they have visited your website. I know some people find this a bit stalkerish, but they did visit your website first. This is done using pixels and a reverse lookup of the visitor via other sites the user has visited. It provides some subtle reminders to come visit again with some high value content. A video with some great content or a white paper that is targeted at a substantial segment of your potential clients can bring prospects back to your site. And no, I do not believe Alexa is "listening" and then presenting ads on sites you visit but it makes for some great dinner conversation.

Influencer marketing

I learned to leverage influence marketing at one of the startups I launched that helped gyms and studios in the fitness industry with software and marketing. Fitness businesses do not typically have a large marketing budget to reach their customers, so my company needed to get creative. Instead of dropping millions of dollars to reach customers in a city of one million people, we marketed to between 250-1000 influencers who then helped draw in the customers we needed.

It worked amazingly well. This is called "influencer marketing" and is not leveraged nearly enough.

To market the launch of a cryotherapy studio we arranged for a well-known fitness instructor to come by weekly for free cryotherapy and then post on social media a picture of himself inside the cryo chamber (from the head up of course). People flocked from the gym that was right next door to the studio to check out why their favorite instructor was doing cryo. And all it cost was a few free cryo sessions! This concept translates well to software. Find the one person in a large company that everyone knows and listens to and get them to try your product.

Find a well-known industry influencer and have a talk with him/her at a large conference. At IBM with the launch of the Maximo Suite we used Spot, the Boston dynamics dog-robot to perform a visual inspection on stage and then sent a work order directly into Maximo to spotlight our product. We knew this influence worked well when three or more of our competitors brought their own Spot to the same conference over the next couple of years. By this time, we were flying drones along bridges and showing live feeds on stage of cracks and rust of a nearby bridge with the governor of South Carolina onstage. You always have to stay one step ahead of competitors.

Now all these methods are good, but what about public relations? Could it be profitable if your business operates in a popular area and has broader appeal? I watched Tommy Siebel do this masterfully when he spoke as an industry expert on a major news channel. He most likely is using a PR agency to arrange these spotlights or has relationships inside these organizations from past PR efforts. It takes a little effort to get your name and company out there, but once you get the PR flywheel going, it is easy to build on that momentum. Public Relations helps build overall brand recognition for businesses that need to expand their reach. Hiring a PR agency can be a little scary as they typically ask for a monthly retainer and no guarantee that you will get any PR. To be successful with PR you need an agency with the ability to reach the audience that matters to your product.

Takeaways:

- Segment the market until you are a leader in "something."
- If it makes sense for your market and product, utilize influencer marketing. It scales much faster.
- Have a well-communicated marketing calendar for your company to ensure everyone knows what is happening when.
- Just call the buyer of your software.
- Invest in well thought out product pages.

Artifacts:

Download Example Marketing Plan

Download Marketing Metrics

Download Example Marketing Calendar

OPERATIONS AND FINANCE

There are many aspects to operations and finance, but I am only going to cover what I consider the most important areas. The first is having a solid financial model for how the company operates and how it will scale. Although it takes a bit of work to build a financial model, it can and should be used throughout the life of the company to work through funding and growth trajectory. The financial model allows you and your team to run scenarios for not only how the business operates today, but how the business could operate.

The other area that is important is metrics. The list I provide is not exhaustive, but includes the most important metrics to measure how well a software company is operating. Finally, we will cover some of the most important legal aspects of operating a software business. Once again, not exhaustive, but I include the areas one should focus on when operating a software business.

Financial Modeling

I will not be able to 100% show how to do financial modeling in this book, but I would encourage you to leverage the financial model available as an add-on to this book. This is an area where the templates are extremely useful. You have to crack open a model and study it for a while, then create a model or two for yourself. Your life will forever be changed by putting in the effort. Even though one of my degrees is in finance, I do not enjoy financial modeling. But it is critical to what I do every day and I have built numerous models that I adapt and use repeatedly. Additionally, I ensure I have a strong CFO, controller or analyst who is good at modeling on my team. They are hard to find, but essential. Some of them even get excited when you ask them to build a new financial model or run a scenario. Given I cannot substitute the time and effort you need to understand how revenue is modeled in a software company, I am only going to hit on a few essential points. I am also not a CPA so please realize accounting rules can and will change. On the positive side, software revenue recognition GAAP rules have been relatively stable. So, let's look at the following financial elements:

- Revenue Recognition
- Saas Modeling
- Cost and Cash Flow Modeling
- Profitability and Product Pricing
- Scaling

Revenue recognition

You first need to learn how revenue is recognized in a software company. Perpetual revenue can be recognized all upfront. Be sure to exclude maintenance revenue which is recognized over the term of the maintenance contract. Subscription revenue is recognized over the term of the subscription in equal time buckets such as monthly. Term revenue can be a hybrid, a portion of the revenue is recognized upfront and a portion that is equivalent to the maintenance, is recognized over the term. The general rule is: If the revenue is non-refundable, then it can be recognized. This applies even to perpetual revenue.

Also note, if a portion of the software is still being developed and the license is covered in a perpetual license agreement, the portion that still needs to be delivered should not be recognized until the software is delivered and the customer has signed off on it.

SaaS Modelling

The complexity of SaaS modeling involves spreading the revenue over the term of the license. For example, if the term of a license is 12 months then the revenue needs to be allocated over 12 equal monthly amounts. Some SaaS products have upfront implementation services that are sold along with the software so this needs to be allocated over an entirely different term.

If the implementation on average takes three months then this revenue should be allocated over the three months. The cascading of revenue over a term makes a fairly complex spreadsheet. The provided financial model handles this complexity. I chose to provide the most complex example of modeling software revenue. If you grasp this model, all other models will seem easy.

Cost and Cash Flow Modelling

Minimally, you need a model of how your business and software is going to scale from both a cost and cash flow perspective. An experienced software CFO can look at the profit and loss statement (P&L) of any software company and recognize if something is off. The secret to what they are looking for is a typical industry ratio. For example, a SaaS company's gross profit should be between 60-80%. Gross margins should be between 15-20%. The development cost to earnings ratio should be 18% or lower. They are looking for the rule of 40, meaning the growth percentage rate, plus the gross margin, should be 40% or higher. Few companies meet that ratio, but if you fit into that category, you are considered a software rock star.

Profitability and Product Pricing

Understanding cash flow and costs are critical to price a software product. A mismatch in the cost structure can break the assumptions that were made when pricing the product. If you are in finance , read the entire section on product pricing. Twice. Some software companies only become profitable with scale. Others become less profitable as they add more customers. Sometimes the mix of customers is critical to profitability. For example, a SaaS company may lose money on smaller customers, but then become profitable for medium to large customers in a manner that then covers the losses on the low end.

Scaling

Scaling is all about the growth of your company. Run your model out five to seven years to understand how it will scale. A one-year model does not tell enough of what is happening over time and to project how the business will grow. Once you have the five to seven years model it makes running scenarios much easier and you will refer back to it periodically to see if reality matches what you planned. If not, adjust the model. You can also run models that show "what if" scenarios, such as, what if I hired ten sales reps tomorrow? What would these hires do to my revenue and in what time frame?

Key Takeaways:

- Have a financial model for your business.
- Know the basics of what a software P&L should look like.
- Interlink your financial modeling with your product pricing

Artifacts:

Download Example Financial Model for SaaS Software

Download Bottom Up Budget (Cash Burn)

Metrics

Product teams and software executives are inundated with metrics. Knowing which metrics to prioritize for your business is key. Understanding which metrics are in your palette of options is important. At the end of the day, you and your team must choose what makes sense for you and your team. This I am sure will produce some healthy debate as no two teams ever seem to agree on the same metrics. Just like investments in software and business, the software metrics used will vary by life cycle stage. An early-stage business is fanatical about its cash flow and a possible customer acquisition. A mature software business pays more attention to contract renewals and customer retention. Selecting metrics often is based on a current problem in your business, such as providing a timely response to customer requests for enhancements.

With effective measurements in place, software leaders can base decisions on data, and deliver products that both meet (and exceed) the customer's needs and propel the business forward. More advanced software companies go so far as to rally the entire organization around product data as a central resource and shared language ensuring they're measuring the right things.

I typically look at the metrics monthly and make course corrections. I also eliminate a metric if it was not driving an outcome. There is a cost to gathering information and I guard my employees' time, enabling it to be spent on what will drive the business where we want to go.

Before we dig into the individual metrics, it's important to zoom out and understand the different types of metrics at your disposal. Here are six categories to keep in mind:

Sales Metrics: The overall health and productivity of the sales team is measured with this metric. Understanding the value of contract attainment per sales rep and the overall total value of the pipeline of the business is important. Sales is an investment, and the investment needs to produce a return. Overall sales performance can fluctuate over time. Understanding if there are problems with the team is important. And any issues with the product or even the general economy can show up in your sales numbers.

Marketing Metrics: These metrics track the overall performance of the money spent on marketing. Is it yielding results?

Growth Metrics: These metrics are relevant to a company that is utilizing product-led growth as a go-to-market model. In this model, the sign up, conversion and retention rates are critical to the overall sales and revenue of the company.

Financial metrics: Measure the overall health and financial performance of the business in both the short and long term. Financial performance is a result of all of the other company metrics combined. You cannot easily engineer your financial way around bad overall performance. For example, your financial performance measures your product experience's effects on customer retention. Your sales performance is linked to your marketing performance which drives leads for sales (or is converted online for the product-led model).

Product Metrics: This category of metric reflects users' behavior based on the quality of the software. Which features do they use the most? How many users continue to use the product over time? How much downtime did you experience last month? What is the overall NPS (net promoter score) for the solution? These metrics, when viewed as a group, give a picture of the overall state of your product.

Sales Metrics

Attainment - What is the annual sales attainment for each of your sales reps along with the average (current and historical) attainment? Think of this like measuring and tracking the batting average for a baseball player.

Pipeline - What is the total amount of revenue (direct and weighted) for each stage of the sales process? How is it trending? How does it compare to prior years? Look for a downward trend in the sales pipeline as it will spell trouble for revenues.

Bookings - What are the total bookings for your software? Even though this revenue is spread out over months or years, I want to see the total. An increase in bookings means the future will get better. A slow down in bookings means my outlying months and quarters will get worse.

Revenue - Obviously, booked revenue matters. Measure it.

Marketing Metrics

I take a fairly direct approach to marketing because I have been shipping software sold to companies (not consumers). If you ship consumer-oriented software, know the names of potential customers, the name of the person buying the software, who they report to, who their peers (that can refer me to them) are, and who reports to them. This can be a list of 100 companies or 10,000. I then want to track progress on reaching these companies. Sounds easy, right?

Below is a sample set of campaign metrics. You can see that we reached only 10% of the stakeholders (across all industries) and that they were reached via a combination of events, direct mail, letters, emails, and phone calls. Even though we reached only some of the customers, we booked 8 meetings, which then resulted in 6 opportunities. Ideally you also have and also track wins (I am rooting for you!). A good rule of thumb is that you will obtain one win for every 15-20 opportunities that are created (depending on the market segment, this can and will vary, but you should have a conversion ratio in your head and know if it is tracking for your business).

Growth Metrics

Number of Trials (per month) – This metric is useful if trials are offered to know how many customers sign up month over month. It shows progression in the company's pipeline. A current trial is a future upgrade to a paid or premium contract. Not every product demands a trial. To be competitive, at one software company we were pushed to conduct online trials for old software. In the first meeting to discuss this idea, I commented that running trials would be a great way for customers to disqualify our product as their software of choice. I can't say I was always the most popular person on these calls.

Conversion to Paid – Trials are useless unless you can eventually convert trial customers to paying customers. I have seen software companies provide a freemium product, which is basically an unlimited time trial, scratch their heads after three years and wonder what to do with the thousands of customers who were still using their solution for free.

Upgrade to Premium – Many revenue models make financial predictions based on how many customers upgrade to a premium or to an enterprise license. Track this progress.

Request for Enhancement (RFE) Opened in Period – If a customer goes out of their way to give you feedback on your software, it is always a good thing. It gives you the opportunity to improve. I would make providing feedback as easy as possible with a simple screen directly within your software.

Financial Metrics

Net Revenue Retention (NRP): The percentage of revenue retained from your existing customers over a given period. Better said, it is the difference between expansion and churn. NRR is generally expected to be valued above 100 percent with the assumption that you're going to lose some customers. It also assumes you are finding ways to expand the value of existing customers.

Measure NRR by subtracting churn from expansion.

NRR is a valuable metric to track because it encompasses all of revenue, expansion, and churn. Software companies attempt to always increase net revenue retention since it represents key goals of expanding customer revenue and minimizing customer loss. Any serious software company will want to know how much revenue your product is able to generate and retain. Review your net revenue retention each month to recognize any downward changes.

Cash flow – How much cash has been produced (or lost) on a monthly, quarterly, and annual basis. Understanding your overall business model and what makes it work and not work is critical. For example, if your cost of a sale is equal to ten months revenue, then billing your customers monthly will result in the company losing money perpetually. SaaS companies learned this early and introduced a discount to get customers to pre-pay annually. Pay close attention to your cash flow or it will swallow you.

Customer Acquisition Cost (CAC) – What is the total cost of acquiring a customer? Acquiring customers is not free. "Build it and they will come" is rarely a strategy that works. We live in a crowded and noisy world where everyone is trying to gain customers' attention. The CAC determines how long it takes, considering revenue and cash collected, to gain a return on the cost of acquiring a customer. Know your CAC, as your business may not scale and perpetually lose money.

Rule of 40 – Want to look cool and have bragging rights in the software industry? Then achieve the rule of 40. This is the desired status of the annual rate of growth as a percentage plus the profit margin being equal to or greater than 40. Admirable, but not always realistic, especially for large companies. This goal is much easier to attain for a startup than a billion dollar company yet it has been done.

Annual (or monthly) recurring revenue (ARR) – This metric measures the amount of revenue obtained via a subscription (or software maintenance) agreement. Investors value companies with high and growing ARR because the revenue is reliable and unless there are issues with customer churn, the revenue is expected to repeat year over year.

Customer Churn – Churn is the percentage of customers who do not renew subscription agreements. Most SaaS solutions are expected to have an 85% or higher customer renewal rate. At one SaaS company, we had a 0.1% customer churn rate as we only lost one customer in the previous ten years.

Customer Lifetime Value – The lifetime value of a customer is the sum of all the revenue from a customer over the entire life of that customer. This includes both software and services revenue. Many companies are shortsighted and do not think through the value of an existing customer, opting to pursue new customers versus maximizing the value of an existing customer.

Customer acquisition cost (CAC) can show that the cost of obtaining a new customer versus the cost of keeping existing customers happy is sometimes 5 to 1; retaining customers is much less expensive.

Product Metrics

Product Adoption - Measures how many users interact with your product. Monthly active users (MAU) or even better, daily active users (DAU) is commonly used to show upward or downward trends in usage. Tracking this requires "metering" the software to keep track of user metrics. A poor man's approach is to update to the last login date and time on the user record in the software. Snapshot this daily and you have your DAU metric.

Feature Adoption – Tracks how often specific features are used. By understanding how (or if) customers adopt and use your product, you'll have a clear sense of whether the product provides its intended value.

Stickiness – Measures the number of customers who regularly use the product. Understanding why some users are sticky and others are not is key to driving overall adoption of the software.

Usage Growth – Measures how well the product is acquiring and retaining new customers (or users), taking into account how many are leaving.

Product usage growth measures the net effect of your user acquisition and retention efforts. Whether it's achieved by adding new accounts or increasing product usage within existing accounts (or ideally, both).

Feature Requests Completed in Period – A growing backlog of feature requests from customers reveals that a product team is not paying attention to, or doesn't have the resources to respond to, what customers are saying. In any given quarter, I want to see a downward slope of inbound feature requests that are now completed feature requests as compared to feature requests that are newly opened. This downward slope shows I am making fixes/improvements faster than customers are logging them. An upward slope obviously means the product team is not keeping up with the demand. There are times when not keeping up is okay and is the plan. For example, when a product is in the cash cow phase the software is being maintained, but not many features are being added.

Feature Requests Average Days to Respond – How many hours or days from when a customer submits a feature request does it take for your product team to respond? In a large software company, I was shocked when I saw the numbers. In many cases, it was "never."

Key Takeaways:

- Pick metrics that make sense for your business.
- Review periodically which metrics you are capturing and question whether they are the correct measures (at this point and time) and balance against the time and cost to gather the metric.

Legal

I am not a lawyer, therefore, I am only going to give a few bits of advice on the legal side of developing software and from my experience, some of the things you need to pay attention to. It is imperative to have a lawyer who understands intellectual property, software license agreements, and has done plenty of work for a software company. Ideally your lawyer, if you ever plan to sell your company, will have experience with more than one diligence effort as part of an M&A transaction. They should provide a standard software license agreement for you to use with all of your customers. Significantly customizing this agreement for every customer will cause you a lot of heartache down the road if you ever decide to sell the company. Allowing customers to move you onto their paper is also troublesome. They are trying to reduce the amount of work they have to do and, in turn, create a lot of work for you in the future.

Given the software is your company's intellectual property, they should use your agreement. If you were purchasing a product from them, there is no chance they would put a license to their product on someone else's license agreement.

Agreement Types

You will need both a software license agreement and a master services agreement for any services work you bundle with your software. For your website, you will also need a privacy agreement and master terms and conditions. If you have partners who resell your software, you will also need a reseller agreement.

Intellectual Property Rights

Paying attention to who owns what IP is important. You should own all IP related to software investments you make. The easiest way to navigate this with customers is to explain that the customers own their requirements, business processes, and information related to their business. You own any resulting software product that is created using those requirements. Who owns data has also become more important, especially with AI algorithms that use machine learning to derive insight from customers' data, and then train a model that will be used across all of the software companies' customers. In the IoT space, equipment manufacturers decided they owned the data generated by the equipment they sold to you and that companies needed to license or subscribe to this data to gain access to it. This was problematic for many companies who were surprised they did not own the operating data from their own equipment. In one recent example, Zoom, the teleconferencing solution, updated its terms of service to allow Zoom to use information obtained during Zoom meetings in a machine learning model. Large customers started to cancel their subscriptions and Zoom had to retreat on this. Given the amount of data companies like Facebook have used for its own profit for years without any recourse, one has to wonder what caused such a backlash for Zoom, but it cannot be ignored.

Assignment Rights

If you ever plan to sell your company, pay attention to the assignment rights in your contracts. One acquisition was held up for months because the French Military would not assign a single contract (out of hundreds) to the company trying to acquire the company. Possibly because they did not know who had the authority to do this. You want to include a provision in all of your contracts that any contract can be automatically assigned if more than 51% of your company has been purchased. You also do not want to be limited by a wait period, such as 30 days, before you can assign a contractor to someone who has acquired your company. Acquisitions can fall through, for example, after you have notified all customers via a 30-day notification period. This could be a source of embarrassment.

Termination Rights

The last area I will highlight is the termination rights for an agreement. Did you sign a 3-year agreement but allow the customer to cancel the agreement with 30 days' notice? If the answer to that is yes, then you signed a 30-day agreement. Only allow a subscription agreement to be terminated for cause and where cause is defined as some really bad stuff that, if you actually do it, you deserve to have the contract canceled.

Antitrust

Antitrust rules were established to promote healthy competition and to control monopolies. Therefore, you should gain some basic knowledge on antitrust rules in the countries you operate. I am not an antitrust lawyer and the rules can get complicated, but you should still spend some time learning and know the basics. Things like customer lists are considered trade secrets, for example, in the United States. A sales representative you hired who brings over a list of customers, regardless of whether or not they have a non-compete, could be in a lot of trouble and can bring a lot of trouble to your company if they downloaded the entire list from a solution like Salesforce.com before they joined your company. Certain types of collaboration with partners or overly aggressive sales tactics are also considered to be "no bueno" (not good or allowed).

Patents

Last, but not least, is the importance of filing for patent protection. Ideally, you have a patent attorney involved. The most important thing to know is that the capabilities you are attempting to patent have not yet been announced externally unless it was discussed under a Non-Disclosure Agreement (NDA). For something to be patented it should be original and not yet exist prior to the patent being issued. In the US, a provisional patent allows you one year from the filing date to file the full patent. I have used provisional patents so I can launch my product and get it out in the market while obtaining the necessary protection for the idea. In addition to filing your own patents, you should do a patent search to ensure that you are not infringing upon someone else's patent. Just because a patent exists does not necessarily mean it is defensible. For example, I have seen instances where a patent was issued and there was prior art (capability) in the market 10+ years before the patent was issued. Due to the prior art, the patent that was issued may not be defensible. Entire technology entities exisit to acquire patents and sue (mostly large companies) as their primary course of business. I do not know how they sleep at night.

Key Takeaways:

- Be familiar with key legal "gotchas", such as, intellectual property rights, termination rights, agreement types, and antitrust laws.
- Have a lawyer with experience in the software industry train your team on the basics so your entire team has a solid foundation on which to operate your business.
- File for patent protection prior to discussing your idea publicly.

Artifacts:

Download Want to do your own US patent search?

CONCLUSION

Learning to know the "why" of your company and products, along with the life cycle, messaging, talent, and culture, hopefully incentivizes you to take a step back and examine those elements more closely. These elements are "foundational;" if you don't understand them as they relate to your current situation, it's like building a home on quicksand. You could lose it all because you don't know why you exist, whom your product serves, and if you have the talent and structural support to reach your goals.

Once your foundation is set, requirements and design are perhaps the most critical sections. These two areas make up my "secret sauce" for how to get a product to market quickly. Most software companies do not understand and execute product requirements effectively. They do not test the product enough with customers to validate that the features they build are as valuable for the end user as the product team thinks they will be. You cannot *assume* your customer's needs. It sounds intuitive, but unfortunately, time and time again, I have found most companies will determine this information in a vacuum. Something as simple as performing user tests can significantly reduce the cost and time of building your product.

Note that when I speak of getting your product to market quickly, I'm not saying being first is key. In fact, if you reread that section, being first, based on history, can sometimes lead to failure if the market is not ready for or does not want what you're offering. Instead, it's all about timing. You must get the right product to the consumer it serves—it's all about properly aligning the product, consumer, and timing.

None of the above sections discussed are to discount the latter part of the book. Each part of this content is vital to bring a product to the end user and maintain its success throughout the software's life cycle. For example, one of the last sections on metrics provides many ways to take the temperature of your product to determine its performance. Besides launching new software, which can be exciting, you must keep your hand on the pulse of your product's workability throughout the stages of use. You must create fixes and add-on features; some will be requested directly, but some can be revealed through the metrics. The sooner you address these issues and deliver desirable results for the customer, the longer you will have that customer (stickiness).

In the end, there is a vast amount of content in this book, and although you may have digested it initially from beginning to end, the book has been designed as a "go-to" guide. Depending on where your product is in the software life cycle, a portion of this book will assist you in navigating those waters with ease. For example, you will not price a product daily. But having read this guide, the next time you price a product, you can reread that section and develop a winning strategy.

In addition, there are artifacts you can access to assist in specific processes. Although they were not initially designed as a product to accompany this book, they have helped my businesses immensely and are invaluable. My team and I still use this book and the templates (artifacts) as references! They are our go-to approach for getting things done quickly and effectively.

Finally, I wish you endless success and hope you share my book with a friend; of course, only if they do not work for one of your competitors!

REFERENCES

Duke, A. (2018). *Thinking in Bets: Making Smarter Decisions When You Don't Have All the Facts.* Penguin Publishing Group.

Elmer, P. (2014, July 16). *The day Apple's Steve Jobs called IBM's best customers an 'orifice'.* Fortune. Retrieved November 9, 2023, from https://fortune.com/2014/07/16/the-day-apples-steve-jobs-called-ibms-best-customers-an-orifice/

Incose Requirements. (2023, April 4). Incose. Retrieved November 8, 2023, from https://www.incose.org/docs/default-source/working-groups/requirements-wg/gtwr/incose_rwg_gtwr_v4_040423_final_drafts.pdf

Judge, M. (Director). (1999). *Office SPace* [Film]. The Walt Disney Company. (Original work published 1999)

Nadella, S., Shaw, G., & Nichols, J. T. (2017). *Hit Refresh: The Quest to Rediscover Microsoft's Soul and Imagine a Better Future for Everyone.* HarperCollins.

Olson, P. (2015, May 26). *BlackBerry's Famous Last Words At 2007 iPhone Launch: 'We'll Be Fine'*. BlackBerry's Famous Last Words. Retrieved November 10, 2023, from https://www.forbes.com/sites/parmyolson/2015/05/26/blackberry-iphone-book/?sh=1799dfe263c9

Schmalcel, L., & Evans, B. (2016, April 6). *The Joy of Tech comic... Google the Hut pays for placement!* Geek Culture. Retrieved October 9, 2023, from https://www.geekculture.com/joyoftech/joyarchives/2236.html

Sinek, S. (2009). *Start with Why: How Great Leaders Inspire Everyone to Take Action*. Penguin Publishing Group.

Spolsky, A. J. (2007). *Smart and Gets Things Done: Joel Spolsky's Concise Guide to Finding the Best Technical Talent* (1st ed.). Apress.

Sutherland, J., & Sutherland, J.J. (2014). *Scrum: The Art of Doing Twice the Work in Half the Time*. Crown.

Tiger team. (n.d.). Wikipedia. Retrieved November 10, 2023, from https://en.wikipedia.org/wiki/Tiger_team.

Veal, R. (2023, May 11). *How to Define a User Persona [2023 Complete Guide]*. CareerFoundry. Retrieved November 10, 2023, from https://careerfoundry.com/en/blog/ux-design/how-to-define-a-user-persona/

Williams, D. D. R. (2021, June 16). *Apollo 13 Accident.* the NSSDCA. Retrieved November 10, 2023, from https://nssdc.gsfc.nasa.gov/planetary/lunar/ap13acc.html

Yourdon, E. (1997). *Death March: The Complete Software Developer's Guide to Surviving "Mission Impossible" Projects.* Prentice Hall PTR.

My editing team and I worked hard to make sure everything was referenced properly, but just in case we inadvertently missed anything, the most up to date references are available online:

ACKNOWLEDGEMENTS

Soli Deo Gloria

Additional thanks to:

My wife, for proofreading multiple draft and fixing grammatical errors.

To https://selfpublishingschool.com which gave me the structure I needed to get my first book written and Brett Hilker my coach, who kept me accountable and guided me through the entire process

My editor, Celeste Chin, who helped improve the overall flow, readability and structure of The Book on Software. I very much appreciated the help, especially as a first time author!

To my early readers who provided valuable input, Theresa Neil at https://guida.com who leads a design firm I have used repeatedly to launch products, Gary Schwake at https://www.yieldgroup.co/ who leads an amazing firm helping early stage companies, Lisa DeLuca who is an amazing entrepreneur and inventor (she is actually the most prolific female inventor in IBM history), Suzanne Livingston whom I have mentored and who also leads a large development team at IBM but also has a product management background.

ABOUT THE AUTHOR

Joe Berti is a seasoned software executive who has been part of software teams that have brought over 20+ products to market. Having worked in both startups and a fortune 50 company, his approach to managing software has transformed the software industry. Mr. Berti has a passion for launching (or re-launching) software products and dominating the competition in whichever software market he participates in. He has truly mastered the art of managing software teams and products. At the time of publishing this book, he was the CEO and founder of P6 Technologies, a

SaaS-based software solution innovating how Product Life Cycle Assessments are performed on Transportation Fuels and Petrochemicals, helping to create a more sustainable approach to industries that account for 73% of all emissions. Prior to P6, Mr. Berti was Chief Product Officer of IBM's $1.5B + sustainability software unit and led the effort to define the company's product strategy for its customers and its products in this software unit. At IBM, Mr. Berti was responsible for a number of product launches and modernization efforts including the Environmental Intelligence Suite, the Digital Twin Exchange, the Maximo Suite (including newly launched modules Maximo Monitor, Health, Predict, Mobile), the TRIRIGA Suite and the Supply Chain Intelligence Suite. Prior to IBM, Mr. Berti was CEO of Oniqua (sold to IBM in 2018), a globally based software company that helped some of the largest utilities, mining, oil & gas, petrochemical, and manufacturing companies reduce their MRO spare parts inventory by up to 30-50%. Berti was also CEO at Clockwork Solutions (sold to LMI), and also led the launch of the Field Service product suite at Servigistics (sold to PTC). Early in his career he helped launch the SAP practice at Ernst & Young when partners were asking why E&Y even needed an entire practice for SAP (they eventually figured that one out!)

FIND ME ON LINKEDIN

https://www.linkedin.com/in/joeberti/

Can You Please Help Me?

Thank You For Reading My Book!

I really appreciate your feedback and want to hear what you have to say.

I need your input to make the next version of this book and my future books even better.

Please leave me an amazing review on Amazon letting me know what you thought of the book.

Thank you so much!

Joseph G. Berti

Can I Help You?

I love talking software with people in the industry

When I am not busy launching my own software products I would love to connect with you. On a limited basis, I meet with executives or can even do an evaluation of your team or company which will give you a clear list of what you may need to focus on. Find me at the https://thebookonsoftware.com/contact